Mapping Appetite

Mapping Appetite
Essays on Food, Fiction and Culture

Edited by

Jopi Nyman and Pere Gallardo

CAMBRIDGE SCHOLARS PUBLISHING

Mapping Appetite: Essays on Food, Fiction and Culture, edited by Jopi Nyman and Pere Gallardo

This book first published 2007 by

Cambridge Scholars Publishing

15 Angerton Gardens, Newcastle, NE5 2JA, UK

British Library Cataloguing in Publication Data
A catalogue record for this book is available from the British Library

ISBN 1-84718-304-2; ISBN 13: 9781847183040

TABLE OF CONTENTS

Part III: Food, Identity and History

ACKNOWLEDGMENTS

Jopi Nyman's research has been supported by the Academy of Finland (project 205780). Pere Gallardo's contribution to this volume is part of the research carried out under the auspices of the T-CLAA Research Group at the Universitat Rovira i Virgili in Tarragona, Spain.

CHAPTER ONE

INTRODUCTION: SETTING THE TABLE

JOPI NYMAN AND PERE GALLARDO

While the field of food studies was for a long time mainly occupied by anthropologists and ethnologists interested in the study of everyday practices, recent years have witnessed a strong interest in various cultural representations of the culinary, ranging from analyses of food representation in film and literature to cultural readings of recipes, menus, national cuisines and celebrity chefs.[1] Such explorations of the diverse roles of the culinary testify to the increasingly important role that food is gaining in today's Western consumer culture, where global food trends follow each other, transforming people's diets and reconstructing their identities. Thus food, while often considered to be too mundane to be studied, is worth studying because of its crucial role in everyday life and consumption in modes that range from televised cookery shows to mass-produced hamburgers. As Warren Belasco writes in a recent collection of essays on food,

> If we are what we eat, we also are what we don't eat. People moralize constantly about what they will and will not eat. To eat is to distinguish and discriminate, include and exclude. Food choices establish boundaries and borders. In the modern era this process of culinary differentiation may entail major modification of traditional foods; few people today eat exactly

---

[1] See, e.g., Bob Ashley, Joanne Hollows, Steve Jones and Ben Taylor, *Food and Cultural Studies* (London: Routledge, 2004); *Eating Culture: The Poetics and Politics of Food*, ed. Tobias Döring, Markus Heide and Susanne Mühlheisen (Heidelberg: C. Winter, 2003); *Kitchen Culture in America: Popular Representations of Food, Gender, and Race*, ed. Sherrie A. Inness (Philadelphia: University of Pennsylvania Press, 2001); *Reel Food: Essays on Food and Film*, ed. Anne L. Bower (New York: Routledge, 2004).

what their grandparents ate fifty years ago, and many of us also like to cross group boundaries to eat the "Other."[2]

What adds to the attraction of food as an object of study is that that it is not a mere symbol of luxurious life-style or conspicuous consumption—and even such roles are historically contingent and constructed differently in different societies. A good example is the work of the Finnish sociologist Jukka Gronow dealing with the origins of champagne culture in Stalin's Soviet Union in the 1930s:

> In food culture in particular, but also in many other areas of consumption, industrially mass-produced, relatively cheap copies of formerly expensive luxury products came to play an important part in the everyday lives of Soviet citizens, now, thanks to the Communist Party and its great leader, Comrade Stalin, every worker could live like an aristocrat.[3]

The story of caviar and champagne, a crucial part of everyday Russian social life, shows that food is, indeed, a part of national and local traditions, inherited and often invented, linking people to others through rituals, places and memories. In so doing, food links us to our intimate histories and memories of childhood and home—be they painful like Pip's family dinners in Charles Dickens's *Great Expectations* or reassuring, as at the end of Beatrix Potter's "The Tale of Peter Rabbit":[4]

> I am sorry to say that Peter was not very well during the evening.
>   His mother put him to bed and made some camomile tea; and she gave a dose of it to Peter!
>   'One table-spoonful to be taken at bed-time.'
>   But Flopsy, Mopsy and Cotton-tail had bread and milk and blackberries for supper.[4]

It is the aim of this volume to explore the representation of food and the culinary in a variety of cultural texts including post-colonial and popular fiction, women's magazines and food writing. This volume has

---

[2] Warren Belasco, "Food Matters: Perspectives on an Emerging Field," in *Food Nations: Selling Taste in Consumer Societies*, ed. Warren Belasco and Philip Scranton (London: Routledge, 2002), 2.

[3] Jukka Gronow, *Caviar with Champagne: Common Luxury and the Ideals of the Good Life in Stalin's Russia* (Oxford: Berg, 2003), 14. Cf. Ben Rogers, *Beef and Liberty: Roast Beef, John Bull and the English Nation* (London: Vintage, 2004).

[4] Beatrix Potter, *The Complete Adventures of Peter Rabbit* (London: Puffin Books, 1984), 19.

been divided into three parts. The first part, entitled "Food, Fantasy and Fiction," explores the various roles allotted to food in contemporary post-colonial writing. The three articles in this section emphasise the various roles of food in post-colonial writing.

In her article, Inga Bryden discusses the translocation of Indian food in Britain by addressing several literary and visual representations of Indian food in the British imagination. By showing how such foods and their preparation contribute to debates about British-Asian identities, she questions traditional notions of authenticity in the larger contexts of globalization, migrancy and tradition. In Bryden's view, while responses to food articulate a desire to link oneself to past traditions expressed as a nostalgic mood, romanticization is not the only possible mode of response. As shown in her analysis of a short film on samosa making, *A Love Supreme*, directed by Nilesh Patel, the martial art of cooking is linked with memory and home. In a similar vein, the work of the contemporary artists Amrit and Rabindra KD Kaur Singh stems from the conventions of Indian miniature painting but applies such methods to the depiction of scenes in contemporary Indian restaurants in Britain. Such hybrid images tell of the emergence of new intercultural spaces in today's Britain, where eating, as Bryden argues, has become one of the "narratives about cultural identity."

The second article in this section, "Sweet Taste of India: Food Metaphors in Contemporary Indian Fiction in English," by Daniela Rogobete, explores the *topos* of food by analysing the use of food and food metaphors in post-colonial writing from India. In the view of Rogobete, such narratives use food allegorically to address questions of art and culture, the nation and the act of creation. In so doing, they show the subcontinent's special interest in the issue of taste, flavours, spices and sensuality. As Rogobete's readings of texts by such authors as Salman Rushdie, Hari Kunzru, Anita and Kiran Desai, Amitav Ghosh, Bharati Mukherjee and Arundhati Roy show, their narratives create different spaces and identities, offering complimentary views of Indianness and showing its struggle with Western values and traditions.

Lia Blaj-Ward's article on the role of food and cafés in narratives of contemporary urban London by contemporary British writers concludes this section. Blaj-Ward's article considers two novels: Maggie Gee's *The White Family* and Zadie Smith's *White Teeth*. Blaj-Ward observes the everyday life experience of ethnically diverse communities in London through the lens of their respective approach to food and "foodways." Her analysis of cafés as sites of tension for the public-private binary leads her to conclude that there is a dynamic relationship between cultural identity and urban space.

The two articles in Part Two, "Food, Power and the Popular," focus on two genres of popular fiction, the romantic novel and science fiction. In her "Writing the Recipe for Subversion: The Creation of Patriarchy-Defying Communities by Means of Cookery," Miriam López-Rodríguez discusses two novels which, although inscribed in different linguistic and cultural realities (Spanish, Mexico and English, Britain), offer the same recipe for the destruction of tyranny, repression, racism and intolerance, namely, the use of cooking as a labour of love which, in turn, generates more love.

Pere Gallardo's article, "Dr. Frankenstein's Technophobic Diet: 'The Iron Chancellor,' by Robert Silverberg" deals with food disorders from the perspective of science fiction. Gallardo focuses on Silverberg's novelette to discuss two main motifs which he deliberately overlaps: on the one hand, the cultural need to possess a slim, healthy figure much in keeping with social class requirements; on the other hand, the so-called Frankenstein complex, a concept developed by Isaac Asimov. The conclusion is that the main issue of the story is neither the human obsession with body image nor the robot's paranoid behaviour, but the incapacity of humans to behave as responsible consumers. Food and electronic goods are presented as two examples of irresponsible consumerism. Both are typical of bourgeois attitudes where decisions are readily made without contemplating the potential consequences.

"Food, Identity and History," the third part of this volume, deals with the representation of food in three genres of non-fiction: travel writing, women's magazines and the cookery book. In his analysis of Paul Richardson's travel book *Cornucopia: A Gastronomic Tour of Britain*, Jopi Nyman locates its search for an allegedly English culinary tradition with its heritage in the context of a national identity in crisis. In his reading of Richardson's book, Nyman addresses its role as a cultural critique seeking to oppose the notions of standardization and unhealthy diet attached to today's fast food. Furthermore, the article also discusses the construction of an English culinary tradition: Richardson's search for a truly English tradition is not merely a search for the local but a means of reconstructing a tradition in the present. The text abounds with national *topoi* ranging from the literary canon to landscape. It is argued that the national culinary tradition promoted in *Cornucopia* is framed in a narrative of ambiguity: while a distinct English tradition may have existed in the past, the demands of hybridization and globalization peculiar to today's culinary trends cannot be escaped. Subsequently, *Cornucopia* appears to recognize the hybrid present while also lamenting the loss of an allegedly true English culinary tradition.

Eleonora Chiavetta's "Representations of Time in Cookery Articles" is a discourse analytic study of the construction of reading communities in the popular British women's magazine *Good Housekeeping* and its "How To" articles. By using Fairclough's theoretical approach to discourse analysis Chiavetta sets out to explore the relationships between food and time as presented in the cookery section. Chiavetta pays special attention to the connection between food and the rhythm of nature, between time and healthy eating, between past times and eating/cooking, and between modern times and eating/cooking. She concludes that the most recurrent aspect turns out to be the relationship between modern times and eating/cooking as the woman, to whom the articles are addressed, has a new role in society.

The final article in this book, Hélène Le Dantec-Lowry's "Writing Women, Writing Food: African-American Women's Cookbooks in Historical Perspective," seeks to provide a reading of African-American cookery books by women. According to Le Dantec-Lowry, cookbooks make it possible for us to learn about the values of the communities producing and consuming such narratives. While the genre has been dominated by white middle-class women, Le Dantec-Lowry shows that African-American women have been actively involved in culinary writing since the abolition. In her analysis of their writings, she argues that black women's experience of food (cooking, selling and finding it), is intricately linked to survival and is often a means of resistance, partially because of the black (slave) woman's role as a cook. Cookbooks, as Le Dantec-Lowry shows, are also instances of creating cultural memory, as they weave narratives of family and culture into recipes. In so doing, they turn an originally informative genre into a personified and named story where meals are located in personal histories. The cultural work of the cookbooks is to preserve the history of black cooking and show the active role of women involved in the domestic.

Bibliography

Ashley, Bob, Joanne Hollows, Steve Jones and Ben Taylor. *Food and Cultural Studies*. London: Routledge, 2004.

Belasco, Warren. "Food Matters: Perspectives on an Emerging Field." In *Food Nations: Selling Taste in Consumer Societies*. Ed. Warren Belasco and Philip Scranton. London: Routledge, 2002. 2-23.

Bower, Anne L., ed. *Reel Food: Essays on Food and Film*. New York: Routledge, 2004.

Döring, Tobias, Markus Heide and Susanne Mühlheisen, eds. *Eating Culture: The Poetics and Politics of Food*. Heidelberg: C. Winter, 2003.

Gronow, Jukka. *Caviar with Champagne: Common Luxury and the Ideals of the Good Life in Stalin's Russia*. Oxford: Berg, 2003.

Inness, Sherrie A., ed. *Kitchen Culture in America: Popular Representations of Food, Gender, and Race*. Philadelphia: University of Pennsylvania Press, 2001.

Potter, Beatrix. *The Complete Adventures of Peter Rabbit*. London: Puffin Books, 1984.

Rogers, Ben. *Beef and Liberty: Roast Beef, John Bull and the English Nation*. London: Vintage, 2004.

Part I: Food, Fantasy and Fiction

CHAPTER TWO

"AN AROMA OF SPICES [...] MAGNIFIED THE SENSE OF WHAT IT MEANT TO LIVE IN ENGLAND": TRAVEL, "REAL" FOOD AND "MISSHAPEN" IDENTITY

INGA BRYDEN

Tracing and interpreting a food's story is also about mapping a cultural geography; a food is both a product of particular times and places, and part of the process of globalisation. Like "any good biography or travelogue," a food's story reveals a "much bigger story."[1] This chapter focuses on the notion of mobile food or, more particularly, what David Sutton has termed "migrant." [2] food.[ ] Migrant food accompanies people travelling across borders, either literally or metaphorically, is sent from home, or is re-created and re-represented in a different context (the new home or diaspora).[ ] The translocation of a food, its transference to a new context (and on another level its transformation through the process of making), allows us to question its "original" conditions. There is a paradox here, in that the very mobility of food from one place to another renders it a means of crystallising a sense of home, that is, being associated with notions of settlement and multi or cross-cultural expectations. As Susanne Freidberg points out, "food has become the flash point of many different struggles in defence of particular cultural norms."[3]

---

[1] Susanne Freidberg, "Not All Sweetness and Light: New Cultural Geographies of Food," *Social and Cultural Geography* 4.1 (2003): 4.
[2] David Sutton, *Remembrance of Repasts: An Anthropology of Food and Memory* (Oxford: Berg, 2001), 75.
[3] Freidberg, 6.

Whose, or what kind of, "home," though, does a food come to represent? In the act of displacement from a settled context, to migrant, to a new context, the meanings of a food blend (re-enacted in the assembling of ingredients and the alchemy of cooking) and are transformed. At the same time, memory plays a crucial role in relation to food, particularly travelling food: tangible, constant, everyday experiences have the power "to evoke the memories on which identities are formed."[4] The rituals and contexts of food preparation and eating can "mutually reinforce each other,"[5] although some foods have a symbolic power which cuts across these contexts. Indeed, through movement itself, food acquires an "'exotica' that over time becomes labelled as different or normalised."[6]

This chapter will consider a nexus of concerns about displaced and replaced food, ritual and memory, through focusing on recent and contemporary literary and visual representations (produced in a British-Asian context) of specific "Indian" foods. The representations of the locus and preparation of these foods are viewed in the context of cultural debates about, and formations of, British-Asian identity; in other words, the space that "Indian food" occupies in contemporary Britain. The extent to which the textual treatments of a food's locations and dislocations are materially grounded will also be considered, in that migration is an integral part of postcolonial debate concerning the processes of globalisation.

Virinder Kalra has questioned whether the samosa is a symbol of multiculturalism and seamless integration, or a marker of "Indianness," of ethnic difference. Indeed, he argues that "the samosa has come to act as a metonym for the presence of 'Indian food' in the British diet and cultural imagination."[7] In one sense the increased interest in the culture(s) and ethnic diversity of food, through tourism, writing about food and television cookery/lifestyle programmes, as well as wider availability and greater opportunities to eat out, might indicate appreciation of "other" cultures, albeit a vicarious one. "Ethnic cuisine […] is the easiest and most pleasant way to cross ethnic boundaries."[8] Whilst greater consumption of ethnic food might contribute to an increased sense of cosmopolitanism, critics such as Lydia Martens and Alan Warde concede that

[4] Sutton, 74.
[5] Sutton, 16.
[6] Virinder Kalra, "The Political Economy of the Samosa," *South Asia Research* 24.1 (2004): 25.
[7] Kalra, 21.
[8] Pierre Van den Berghe, "Ethnic Cuisine: Culture in Nature," *Ethnic and Racial Studies* 7.3 (1984): 396.

understandings of multiculturalism are still limited.[9] In the case of the samosa though, its ability to cross cultural boundaries comes from its flexible filling and its symbolism as a food for all classes.

This raises related issues, however, to do with consumption and authenticity: for example, does the re-exportation of chicken tikka masala function symbolically as a subversion of national identity? In *Balham to Bollywood*, Chris England refers to the status of chicken tikka masala as a British national dish, whereas he can find no sign of it in India: "hysterically, it is being exported from Britain to India and Bangladesh to satisfy the demands of frustrated British holidaymakers."[10] The "colonial" activity of "going for a curry" has become, since the 1990s television (following radio) comedy series *Goodness Gracious Me*, the postcolonial "going for an English." The recent marketing in Britain of Indian restaurants under the auspices of "Masala World" insists on the "realness" of the "street" food served on one hand and on the other, on colonial heritage and a rajification of food. Through the Masala Zone restaurants, the business owners sought to create stylish, affordable restaurants serving "real" Indian food in London.[11] The website claims that dishes are "prepared authentically, as in Indian homes" and that they hail "from the homes of regional gourmet families, Maharajas' palaces and humble wayside stalls," whilst at the same time emphasising that the restaurants are "sophisticated, captivating" environments and that the menu reflects food trends in today's India.[12]

In considering the movement of food in terms of the cycle of production and consumption, visibility is a key factor; seeing, or being mindfully connected to, the hand that cooks can be an assertion of the notion of homemade (or misshapen) authenticity. Are British-Asian women represented as occupying a domestic (often conflated with traditional) space and as invisible in the public space of the restaurant?[13] Kalra questions whether, in a diasporic context, production of samosas in the home "can ever be an unalienated act of love,"[14] or whether the

---

[9] Lydia Martens and Alan Warde, *Eating Out: Social Differentiation, Consumption and Pleasure* (Cambridge: Cambridge University Press, 2000), 83.
[10] Chris England, *Balham to Bollywood* (London: Sceptre, 2002), 107-8. England claims that there are 48 distinct recipes for chicken tikka masala in circulation in Britain.
[11] The business is owned by Namita Panjabi and Ranjit Mathrani of Chutney Mary and Veeraswamy, the oldest surviving Indian restaurant in the UK.
[12] http://www.realindianfood.com (accessed April 5, 2007).
[13] Uma Narayan, "Eating Cultures: Incorporation, Identity and Indian Food," *Social Identities* 1.1 (1995): 75.
[14] Kalra, 22.

women who make them are always defined as outside the labour process. In Blair's Britain the role of the samosa-maker as entrepreneur allows a shift from home as a site for the maintenance of both Indian national culture (in the face of the colonising British) and diasporic culture (in the context of contemporary Britain). The home can thus "potentially be created," according to Kalra, as a space "in but not of the world."[15]

> Engaging with making a samosa at home though should not imply brown hands working on flour in some time-honoured, word of mouth, generational treasured recipe, with great-grandmother whispering the secrets of the recipe to daughters yet to come.[16]

This is the image of Indian food, Kalra argues, that is reinforced by contemporary Indo-Anglian literature. Interestingly, similar criticism about the nostalgic, therefore "inauthentic," rendering of food and food preparation has been levelled at Indo-Anglian literature as a genre. Salman Rushdie points out that such literature has been criticised as a postcolonial anomaly and as inauthentic, whereas English has become a naturalised subcontinental language. Writers born in India but living outside it are castigated "for being the literary equivalent of MTV culture, of globalising Coca-Colonisation."[17]

Many literary texts do indeed emphasise the matrilineal ritual of food preparation as invoked in Kalra's description; a process nostalgically framed as memory. Bulbul Sharma's short stories, for example, collected in *The Anger of Aubergines: Stories of Women and Food* (1997), highlight an appreciation of women's craft and the skill involved in, say, slicing onions:

> The others would make room for her in the crowded kitchen and sometimes even stand around watching her as she chopped and sliced with expertise. She became so good at her craft that she could even look up and still slice layers of onions as fine as paper.[18]

In the story "Food to Die For," the slow, precise, silent movements of a group of women preparing food in the kitchen are like a "secret ritual":

---

[15] Kalra, 32.

[16] Kalra, 26.

[17] Salman Rushdie, "Introduction," in *The Vintage Book of Indian Writing 1947-1997*, ed. Salman Rushdie and Elizabeth West (London: Vintage, 1997), xiii.

[18] Bulbul Sharma, *The Anger of Aubergines: Stories of Women and Food* (New Delhi: Kali for Women, 1997), 56.

It was still dark when I heard my grandmother and Gopal in the kitchen. Gradually, as dawn began to break the other women joined them. They worked silently in the dim light as if performing a secret ritual, their movements slow and precise and their silhouettes shifting and merging like ghosts dancing [...] Two women sat on the floor with a flat plate of flour—while one kneaded the dough the other kept pouring small amounts of water. They did not speak to each other but just nodded together every time the water was poured as if taking part in a pantomime.[19]

The figure of the cook has a particular resonance in the reconstructed memories of India or other place of growing up, not just in recent literary fiction, but in contemporary memoirs, Indian cookery books and food magazines. From a distance, from the new home, the writers reconnect to a particular place via memories of food and childhood. Chitrita Banerji recalls in *Gastronomica*:

This ritual of cutting, called kutno kota, was almost as important as the daily rituals carried out for the household gods. Some of my fondest childhood memories involve sitting near my grandmother on the floor of the large central space in her Calcutta house as she peeled and sliced the vegetables for the day's main afternoon meal.[20]

In Amitav Ghosh's *In an Antique Land*, it is the cook, a mesmerising storyteller who learnt his skills on the river steamers, who looms large in the narrator's memories of a childhood spent in a residential suburb in Dhaka. "After his coming, the food in our house had become legendary amongst our family's friends."[21] The cook engenders fascination, awe and fear. Similarly, in Kamila Shamsie's *Salt and Saffron* (2000), about Pakistani immigrant culture, a cook of legendary, almost magical, powers, crystallises memories of home. On a plane to Karachi, the narrator remembers the culinary (rather than the religious) significance of the festival of Ramzan: people tried to steal the utensils belonging to her Aunt's cook, to try and recreate the taste. "The delight was in his hand."[22] Here, the hand is symbolic of individualism, the art of the homemade, and the sensuality of food. Such factors are often highlighted by the

---

[19] Sharma, 112-3.
[20] Chitrita Banerji, "The Bengali Bonti," *Gastronomica: The Journal of Food and Culture* 1.2 (2001): 23.
[21] Amitav Ghosh, "Nashawy," in *The Vintage Book of Indian Writing*, ed. Salman Rushdie and Elizabeth West (London: Vintage, 1997), 418.
[22] Kamila Shamsie, *Salt and Saffron* (London and New York: Bloomsbury, 2000), 74.

proprietors and cooks of the newer Indian restaurants in Britain. The Rasa restaurants are perhaps representative of a situation where "the British are finally waking up to the fact that there is more to Indian food than chicken tikka masala and flock wallpaper."[23] In the introduction to *The New Tastes of India* (with a foreword by Jamie Oliver), Das Sreedharan, founder of Rasa, recalls waking at 4 am to watch his grandfather cook in the smoke-filled kitchen and conjure up a myriad of tastes.

In common with a growing number of fictional narratives about food, texts such as Sharma's *The Anger of Aubergines* and Rohan Candappa's *Picklehead: From Ceylon to Suburbia* (2006) incorporate recipes.[24] Recipes are integral to the narrative and are used as a means both of excavating family histories characterised by movement and of imparting a secret to be shared with the reader. This is particularly evident in *Picklehead*, subtitled "a memoir of food, family and finding yourself," in which the author, growing up a second-generation Asian immigrant in 1970s South London, traces his family's itinerant history and muses on the links between food and notions of home. Candappa's epiphany comes when he buys a jar of Sainsbury's korma sauce and realises that he "has lost something," whilst Britain, where "vindaloo" had become the refrain of the England football team's World Cup song, has gained something.[25] Not sure what it is that he has lost, Candappa is convinced that "if you're the child of immigrant parents, the food you eat at home is more than just the food you eat at home"[26]—it is a link to a whole series of past places and people.

Recipes emblematise these links. As Janet Floyd and Laurel Forster suggest, recipes should be read as cultural texts, in relation to debates about lifestyle and national identity; more than instructions for producing meals, they evoke the "elaborate scene of home."[27] Recreated in a literary text, Candappa's mother's recipe for Chicken Kyaukswe, for example, is inseparable from her storytelling (and listening) skills and the attention-grabbing techniques of the wandering street-sellers in Burma. The author

---

[23] Das Sreedharan, *The New Tastes of India* (London: Headline, 2001), inside cover.

[24] Another example is Laura Esquivel, *Like Water for Chocolate*, trans. Carol Christensen and Thomas Christensen (London: Black Swan, 1993).

[25] This is similar to Narayan's "perfect post-colonial moment" on finding that "curry" derived from the Tamil, "kari." See Narayan, 65.

[26] Rohan Candappa, *Picklehead: From Ceylon to Suburbia* (London, Ebury Press, 2006), 10.

[27] Janet Floyd and Laurel Forster, "Introduction: The Recipe in Its Cultural Contexts," in *The Recipe Reader: Narratives, Contexts, Traditions*, ed. Janet Floyd and Laurel Forster (Aldershot: Ashgate, 2003), 1.

playfully addresses the reader: "don't share the recipe with anyone else. Just share the dish, and let them be blown away by your artistry."[28] Recipes are not always treasured matrilineal secrets though: in Sharma's story "Sandwiched," they are the site of cultural and familial struggle, articulating the competition between a wife and her mother-in-law to feed the husband/son. Whereas the wife frantically collects recipes to use, the mother-in-law prides herself on not needing a recipe book. Recipes also narrativise the movement and transformation of food across cultures, places and times. Kedgeree is, according to David Burton:

> a prime example of how one recipe can eventually transmute into another, for, aside from the rice, this delightful Anglo-Indian jumble of smoked fish, rice and chopped egg bears no relation to its parent recipe of the same, or similar name.[29]

The predominant tone, however, of literary descriptions of food preparation and recipes, is nostalgia! Such desire invoked by distance (in personal geographical or historical terms) is shared with contemporary Indian cookery books whose commentaries also locate food in a specific space (the street, or the mobile space of a train carriage) and attempt to fix a sense of home. Madhur Jaffrey's books and television programmes had a key role in bringing Indian cooking into the British household. The samosa recipe in *Madhur Jaffrey's Indian Cookery* is contextualised by the comment that

> Indians love to munch [...] whether they are on buses, trains, cinema houses or in parks, they can be spotted opening up newspaper cones, unwrapping tea-cloth bundles or easing eager hands into terra cotta pots.[30]

This sentiment is echoed in Sharma's story "Train Fare" which celebrates the memory of meals being cooked on long train journeys. In the mid-late nineteenth century, as C. P. Edmund Hull reminds us, travellers on trains in India would "carry what provision is required for the road with them" and well into the twentieth century, when stations had different dining rooms on the platform, "anybody with any sense avoided the European

---

[28] Candappa, 30.

[29] David Burton, *The Raj at Table: A Culinary History of the British in India* (London: Faber, 1993), 83. "Khichri," as commonly understood in Indian cookery, is a combination of rice and dal boiled with spices.

[30] Madhur Jaffrey, *Madhur Jaffrey's Indian Cookery* (London: BBC Books, 1982), n.p.

restaurant."[31] In the more contemporary train carriage setting of Sharma's text, passengers are in danger of being crowded out by food and utensils. "Gopal looked around helplessly. His wife, having eaten six pooris and halwa from a stranger's kitchen, now lay curled up on the upper berth."[32] Gopal recounts how:

> Sometimes, on long journeys, she [his mother] brought a tiny stove along and cooked meals on the train. The servant would chop the vegetables and Gopal could still remember how his knife would waver as the train gathered speed and pieces of carrots and potatoes would roll off the plate into dark corners under the berths.[33]

A key component of remembering is taste and smell, or synesthesia. As Sutton points out, the sensory is "an embodied aspect of creating the experience of the whole"[34] and it is this aspect which is particularly distinctive in literature and cookery texts about Indian food. In introducing samosas, Jaffrey suggests that they taste best when eaten in the street.

Other literary texts, however, do not present such a romanticised, even exoticised picture. In Anita Desai's *Fasting, Feasting* (1999) Uma is burdened both by not knowing how to make samosas and, after marriage to a fraudulent husband, by the oppressive rituals of having to learn "how to cut vegetables in pieces of exactly the same size, how to grind spices into a wet paste and how to tell one dhal from another."[35] Githa Hariharan's *The Remains of the Feast*, like Desai's text, reminds us that "Indian" foods in an Indian or British context can have complex significations of religion, caste and taste. Ratna, studying to become a doctor, goes in search of taboo foods (including samosas made by non-Brahmin hands) to feed her dying, vegetarian great-grandmother's cravings; for coke, bhel-puri, fried bread, raw onions and meat "from the fly-infested bazaar nearby."[36] After her great-grandmother's death, Ratna haunts the dirty spaces of food production, eating in an effort to revive her dead relative—and gives herself diarrhoea; her great-grandmother's revenge. "I haunt the dirtiest bakeries and tea-stalls I can find every evening. I search for her, my sweet great-grandmother, in plate after plate

---

[31] Burton, 44-5.

[32] Sharma, 67.

[33] Sharma, 71.

[34] Sutton, 102.

[35] Anita Desai, *Fasting, Feasting* (London: Vintage, 1999), 93.

[36] Githa Hariharan, "The Remains of the Feast," in *The Vintage Book of Indian Writing 1947-1997*, ed. Salman Rushdie and Elizabeth Wilson (London: Vintage, 1997), 426.

of stale confections, in needle-sharp green chillies, deep-fried in rancid oil."[37]

A striking visual representation of food production in the home is the short film *A Love Supreme* (2001), directed by the architect Nilesh Patel, which illustrates in monochrome the eight stages, or rituals, involved in making a samosa[38] The shot stays on a woman's (the director's mother's) hands, highlighting the process itself, rather than an individual identity and there is no voiceover, just white on black titles which announce each stage. The camera also avoids lingering on kitchen equipment, thus resisting the cult of globalised cooking as lifestyle. Indeed, Stephanie Argy regards the film as "really about the love that goes into those dishes"[39] and the selflessness of hand-prepared food, a position reinforced by the final credit: "Dedicated to my Mother, her Mother, and your Mother."

It is tempting, then, to see *A Love Supreme* as a timeless celebration of a skilled craft, which in one sense it is. This impression is partly undercut, though, if we know that the director's mother arrived in Britain from Gujarat in 1966 and, due to a life working as a machinist in knitwear factories, developed rheumatoid arthritis. Shot in the style of the fight scenes in Martin Scorsese's *Raging Bull* (1980), cooking is transformed into a martial art. Patel himself sees it as a feminist film, one which stylises "creation rather than destruction, decorated female palms rather than gloved male fists, rolling and folding rather than jabbing and punching, but will still celebrate skill, speed and accuracy."[40] Patel's short film is an example of texts which emphasise the production, travelling and circulation of a specific cultural image within a global market, arguably offering up "the subversive potential of an 'ethnic' counter-culture of images, within the prevailing western discourse of the 'other.'"[41]

In utilising the subversive potential of the image of the samosa, Patel destabilises Kalra's assertion that cultural texts tend to reinforce the

---

[37] Hariharan, 429.

[38] Nilesh Patel, dir., *A Love Supreme*, Les Beauchistes 2001. The title refers to the black American jazz musician John Coltrane's album (in collaboration with Ravi Shankar) and the film's music is a mixture of Bollywood, classical Indian, Indian samples, and drum 'n' bass. Screened in front of *Monsoon Wedding* and *The Warrior*, the film has won prizes at international short film festivals, toured India for the British Council in March 2003 and had its television premiere on BBC4, June 21, 2003.

[39] Stephanie Argy, "Short Takes: A Loving Tribute to a Mother's Cooking," *American Cinematographer* (2002): 98.

[40] Press notes given to the author by Nilesh Patel.

[41] Clare Melhuish, "The Cultural Imagery of Patel's *A Love Supreme*," *The Architects' Journal* 2.9 (2001): 12.

romanticised, domesticated, ritualised image of Indian food. What is also striking is the extent to which literary texts debunk the myth that there is an authentic, fantastical, pure curry in India or that, in a diasporic context, food from "home" can only be recreated as an unadulterated memory, or as a pure form which allows nostalgia to flourish. Indian food has always been a product of cultural integration; what Uma Narayan terms its "odd nature" reflected in the "cracked" nature of contemporary India.[42] It lacks the clear referent in India that it has in western contexts. Conversely, more western-style fast foods are likely to be regarded as trendy in India and a signifier of social status, in contrast with their more "plebeian place in western contexts." [43] The tangled cultural assumptions and ideologies surrounding food are well illustrated in Firdaus Kanga's *Trying to Grow*:

> "God! Don't tell me you're one of those [..] The kind who have Kraft cheese for breakfast. Plumrose sausages for lunch, whoop it up in their imitation Dior clothes, end the day on caviare and champagne—all imported, of course. They don't enjoy anything Indian."
> "I think that's the kind of life I'd like," I said.
> "You're a fool if you lean on that sort of thing to have fun."[44]

The "lasting" influence of British food in India extends only, in Burton's summary, to: "biscuits (packed in solid corrugated cardboard, with brand names like Britannia), second-rate white soda bread, omelettes, and English breakfasts of porridge, boiled eggs, tea, toast and marmalade."[45] In Saadat Hasan Manto's *Toba Tek Singh* such "authentic" English breakfasts are to be desired. Two Anglo-Indians are "worried about their changed status after independence [...] Would breakfast continue to be served or would they have to subsist on bloody Indian chapatti?"[46]

Indian food, particularly since the rise of the Indian restaurant in all its incarnations, can be synonymous with localised senses of home, where Britain is home. In his part travelogue, part memoir, Alex Kapranos writes how he misses "a good [Glaswegian] curry" when he is on tour with the band Franz Ferdinand. Having delivered takeaways for Mother India's Café, Kapranos's memories are filled with the smell of hot spices. More than anything "it became the vivid taste of homesickness—a distant desire,

---

[42] Narayan, 71.
[43] Narayan, 69.
[44] Firdaus Kanga, "Trying to Grow," in *The Vintage Book of Indian Writing 1947-1997*, ed. Salman Rushdie and Elizabeth West (London: Vintage, 1997), 332.
[45] Burton, viii.
[46] Saadat Hasan Manto, "Toba Tek Singh," in *The Vintage Book of Indian Writing 1947-1997*, ed. Salman Rushdie and Elizabeth West (London: Vintage, 1997), 26.

unattainable. Not HP sauce, Tetley tea or Yorkshire puddings, but Saag Paneer."[47] Nostalgia is made manifest: the literal translation, through taste and consumption, of homesickness.[48]

Vesta Curry, launched in 1961 by Batchelors, may be included in the "Noshtalgia" list of *The Guardian's* "50 Years Food and Drink: Food Summer Special," but memories are fallible, food changes shape in cooking and eating, and recipes are always ripe for adaptation. Like the Anglo-Indian concoction curry powder, chutneys and pickles have been adapted to suit European tastes at different times. In Desai's *Fasting, Feasting*, the ladies in a Christian mission order peanut butter and pickle relish from Landour, having taught a local grocer how to make them:

> "Pickle relish?" one lady enquires, through sticky lips and teeth coated with peanut butter.
> "Yes, pickles like you have, but sweet, not hot."
> "Sweet pickles?" the lady explodes with astonishment.[49]

Jam or chutney also symbolises the ambiguity and inability of food to be contained in neat categories, in Arundhati Roy's *The God of Small Things* (1997). The "banned" banana jam made at Rahel's grandmother's pickle factory is an "ambiguous consistency," "neither jam nor jelly"; furthermore, it comes to represent family members breaking the rules "that lay down who should be loved and how," frustrating the need to classify in a broader context.[50]

Conflicting family and cultural loyalties are articulated in and through food in *Fasting, Feasting*, where Desai uses the middle-class Arun's story to explore, I would argue, the mobility of food versus the stasis of apparently clashing cultural values. Growing up in the bosom of a traditional middle-class Indian family, where daily arguing over what meals to order from the family cook is a comforting parental ritual, Arun's feeding is monitored with precision. Meat, in this context, equals progress, along with "cricket and the English language," [51] an assumption confounded by Arun turning out to be vegetarian. During a summer residing with the Patton family in Massachusetts, the student Arun encounters frozen food and a "frozen" culture, alien to the culture back

---

[47] Alex Kapranos, *Sound Bites: Eating on Tour with Franz Ferdinand* (London: Penguin, 2006), 37.
[48] From the Greek, nostos (return home) and algos (pain).
[49] Desai, 115.
[50] Arundhati Roy, "Things Can Change in a Day," *Granta: India! The Golden Jubilee* 57 (1997): 258.
[51] Desai, 32.

home. Markets have chilled, controlled atmospheres, vegetables "seemed as unreal in their bright perfection as plastic representations"[52] and Mrs Patton "stops, a can of plum tomatoes in her hand, and does not seem to know what to do next. She is frozen."[53] Moreover, the smell of barbequing meat defines the suburbs.

The food rituals of western culture are represented in Desai's text as equally farcical as those of India, and yet the different foods enshrine contrasting values, where "real" food is ugly, homemade, flawed and tasty, not sterile and packaged:

> No, [Arun] had not escaped. He had travelled and he had stumbled into what was like a plastic representation of what he had known at home; not the real thing—which was plain, unbeautiful, misshapen, fraught and compromised—but the unreal thing—clean, bright, gleaming, without taste, savour or nourishment.[54]

Craving what he had taken for granted, Arun tries to cook dhal and fails (having never seen his mother cook), concluding that in both cultural contexts he is caught in the "sugar-sticky web of family conflict."[55] Desai reveals that in spite of the globalization of food, its appropriation in the interests of satisfying and expressing emotional needs is constant: "But what is plenty? What is not? Can one tell the difference?"[56]

Food sharing across geographical and cultural divides is supposed to consolidate social and familial ties.[57] In Sara Suleri's fictional memoir *Meatless Days* (as in Candappa's *Picklehead*) meals "speak over and across the separation of our lives"[58] and memories of these are the basis for constructing identity. In New York among Pakistanis, noting that "expatriates are adamant, entirely passionate about such matters as the eating habits of the motherland,"[59] the narrator goes back "past a thousand different mealtimes" and starts to reconstruct the parable of the kapura[60] (sweetbreads) eaten in Lahore. However, returning to Lahore in actuality

---

[52] Desai, 184.
[53] Desai, 162.
[54] Desai, 185.
[55] Desai, 195.
[56] Desai, 214.
[57] Van den Berghe, 390.
[58] Sara Suleri, "Meatless Days," in *The Vintage Book of Indian Writing 1947-1997*, ed. Salman Rushdie and Elizabeth West (London: Vintage, 1997), 302.
[59] Suleri, 303.
[60] Suleri, 307-8.

(and in memory) things are "out of place" ("safe" food items vanish or return re-packaged or adulterated):

> Items of security—such as flour or butter or cigarettes or tea—were always vanishing, or returning in such dubiously shiny attire that we could barely stand to look at them. We lived in the expectation of threatening surprise: a crow had drowned in the water tank on our roof, so for a week we had been drinking dead-crow water and couldn't understand why we felt so ill; the milkman had accidentally diluted our supply of milk with paraffin instead of water; and those were not pistachios, at all, in a tub of Hico's green ice-cream.[61]

Such "promiscuous blendings" symbolise "the fear that food will not stay discrete but will instead defy our categories of expectation in what can only be described as a manner of extreme belligerence."[62]

The parable, then, is ultimately concerned with "the imaginative extravagance of food and all the transmogrifications of which it is capable."[63] In this context, the small matter of frying *shami kebabs* "refusing to cohere into their traditional shape" takes on a greater significance. "Never mind," the narrator says, "we'll just call them Kuwaiti *kebabs* and then no one will know they look peculiar."[64]

Like Arun in *Fasting, Feasting*, the narrator of *Meatless Days* tries to learn to cook in the new homeland, away from the (sometimes stifling) security of home and family. The particular form of food which, in many literary texts, eludes recreation and yet is most evocative of childhood and a specific locale, is snacks. The narrator remembers most roaming with her girlhood friends in search of the best *gol guppa* (a small hollow oval of light pastry, dipped in a fiery sauce) vendor in town: "I have never located an equivalent to [*gol guppas*] or their culinary situation. They are an outdoor food, a passing whim, and no one would dream of recreating their frivolity inside her own kitchen."[65] Snacking marks time and is the catalyst for memories of youth and sensual pleasure.

It is clear, then, that cooking food is not necessarily a direct link to some kind of authentic sense of home; the process might instead work to construct a new or hybrid identity. In Amit Chaudhuri's *Afternoon Raag* (1993) the narrator notes of his fellow Oxford student and friend, Sharma: "He was kitchen-friendly as well, and spent a good amount of time

---

[61] Suleri, 309.
[62] Suleri, 309-10.
[63] Suleri, 314-5.
[64] Suleri, 320.
[65] Suleri, 319.

making food that emitted an aroma of spices that magnified the sense of what it meant to live in England."[66] Even though the sense of Englishness is enhanced, paradoxically, through the recreation of the cooking smells of home in India, Sharma does not adopt a new identity, "as many city-educated Indians do in England." Contrastingly, the narrator falls between two worlds "clinging to my Indianness, or letting it go, between being nostalgic or looking toward the future."[67] His memories of Bombay do include his mother preparing pithhas, but they also incorporate "American hamburger and chop-suey" and "the local bhelpuri with its subversive smells of the narrow, spice-smelling streets of west Bombay."[68] Daily life in Oxford already resonates with recognisable, diverse cultural tones: in the Bangladeshi shops on Cowley Road the aisles are "stacked with boxes of chilli powder, packets of dried fruit, jars of pickles, and imported vegetables—roots and tubers—with the flecked soil of Bangladesh still upon them"[69] whilst the coffee served in St Giles' Café has a "scorched South Indian flavour."[70]

The calendar pictures of gods and goddesses in Sharma's room remind *Afternoon Raag's* narrator of roadside kitchens and roasting chickpeas. The British-Asian artists Amrit and Rabindra KD Kaur Singh develop this association further, visualising and adapting details of food preparation and cooking, and to an extent secularising the role food has in relation to prayer, as represented in Indian miniature painting for example. The twins, who were brought up as Sikhs in Liverpool, have explained how they learnt the importance of the observation of such rituals in Britain, and the underlying values, in India. The iconography of the temple is important and the household, in contemporary Britain, is perceived as the centre of debate, both sacred and secular.[71]

The twins' paintings thus participate in cultural debates about East and West through the representation of food in everyday contexts (the household as the centre of debate) and through translating the language of traditional Indian miniature painting in order to challenge the constructed "norms" of social behaviour. *All Hands on Deck* (1997) depicts the ritual preparation of food for a wedding, in an outdoor, courtyard environment

---

[66] Amit Chaudhuri, *Afternoon Raag* (London: Vintage, 1998), 127.

[67] Chaudhuri, 128-9.

[68] Chaudhuri, 24.

[69] Chaudhuri, 36.

[70] Chaudhuri, 24.

[71] Joan Bakewell, interview with Amrit and Rabindra KD Kaur Singh, *Belief*, Radio 3, December 27, 2002.

which mixes the mundane and the paradisiacal.[72] Although hard work is involved, the tasks are shared by the generations and accompanied by gossip and jokes; the institution of the extended Asian family is celebrated, whilst the notion of western individualism is discarded, symbolised by the Union Jack cardboard box mingling with the rubbish in the bottom right-hand corner of the painting.

The central focus of *Mr Singh's India* (1999/2000),[73] commissioned by the Glasgow Gallery of Modern Art, is a scene inside one of Glasgow's most well-known Indian restaurants, Mr Singh's India. The restaurant's name indicates that it belongs to the "third stage" of the changing power relationship between Indian restaurants and British society, according to Ziauddin Sardar and Borin Van Loon's analysis, whereby new ethnicities are revealed and Indians are invited to eat Indian.[74] Diners in the depicted restaurant include the artists themselves, Scottish sports and entertainment celebrities, Sikh boys in Scottish football strip, William Wallace, the Scottish freedom fighter, and his Punjabi counterpart Maharaja Ranjit Singh. The painting has been interpreted as a "perfect example of Glasgow's cross-cultural vibrancy," in the symbolic context of ongoing historical and cultural links between Scotland and the Punjab. At the least, it articulates the ways in which diasporic communities carry cultural traditions with them to "create a home from home which is secure in its own identity whilst in the midst of a new and, often, alien environment."[75]

Contrastingly, the row of Indian restaurants described in *Afternoon Raag* specifically recalls an earlier phase of the Indian restaurant in Britain, when Raj and colonial connections were very much in evidence:

> honest Englishmen sat being served among fluted armrests and large, mendacious pictures of palm-trees and winding rivers, helplessly surrendering to an inexhaustible trickle of eastern courtesy; everything, including the waiters, smelled strongly of mint and fenugreek. The restaurants were seedy, but generous with life; and from the silvery letters

---

[72] Poster colour, gouache and gold dust on mount board. 52 x 74.5 cm. Rabindra KD Kaur Singh, Twin Studio Collection, http://www.singhtwins.co.uk /gal_page2.htm (accessed August 25, 2006).
[73] Poster colour, gouache and gold dust on mount board. 59.7 x 76.2 cm. Amrit and Rabindra KD Kaur Singh, Glasgow Gallery of Modern Art, http://www.singhtwins.co.uk /gals/public/singh.htm (accessed August 25, 2006).
[74] See Ziauddin Sardar and Borin Van Loon, *Introducing Cultural Studies* (New York: Totem Books, 1998).
[75] http://www.singhtwins.co.uk/gals/public/singh.htm (accessed April 11, 2007).

of the sign outside, to the decor within, was a version of that style called the "oriental."[76]

The question of the authenticity of Indian restaurants and the food served therein still exercises cultural commentators and restaurant reviewers. Reviewing the west London restaurant Benares, Matthew Fort notes approvingly the modern décor (as opposed to the gilded effects of older interiors) and the specifically-spiced dishes (rather than an "all-purpose glop"). At the same time, the restaurant has not adopted Europeanised presentation techniques which leaves Fort wondering, "God knows if it was authentic, but it was traditional, if you see what I mean."[77] Authenticity has been utilised more recently by Indian restaurants as a sign of resistance, argue Sardar and Van Loon, and as an assertion of identity. It might be associated with a particular dish, such as balti, or with the notion of home or hand-cooked.[78] Away from home, diners desire the dining experience to represent an authentically different cultural experience: as Van den Berghe wrily comments, "every good tourist resents the presence of his own kind."[79]

Sitting at her "favourite table" in the restaurant Tandoori Nights (owned by the Hassan family who came to Britain in the 1960s), Monica Ali recalls how "curry" has moved from the home to the legitimising space of the restaurant; when her family first moved to Bolton from Dhaka, "we didn't really eat out. Curry was just something we ate every day at home. You could smell it all the way down the street." In this case, then, the restaurant dishes, cooked individually, recreate a home from home; "when I first visited I was eating the curry and naan with my fingers."[80]

Food features in Ali's novel *Brick Lane* (2003) as a signifier of multiculturalism (the street sells "bits and pieces"[81] from all over the world); of ethnic difference (the husband, arriving in hospital with home-cooked Indian food is stared at, because of the smell), and of small acts of rebellion (Nazneen, the heroine, puts chopped raw chillies in her husband's sandwiches to take to work).

---

[76] Chaudhuri, 36-7. Britain's first Indian restaurant, the Hindostanee Coffee House (1809) in Portman Square, London, catered for enthusiastic colonials rather than Indian ex-patriots. See Matthew Sweet, *Inventing the Victorians* (London: Faber, 2001), 107.

[77] Matthew Fort, "Eating Out," *The Guardian Weekend*, August 16, 2003, 73.

[78] See Sardar and Van Loon.

[79] Van den Berghe, 394.

[80] Monica Ali, "My Favourite Table," *Observer Food Magazine*, August 2003, 47.

[81] Monica Ali, *Brick Lane* (London: Doubleday, 2003), 81.

Revitalising food as an object of everyday life means that culinary practices become, in and of themselves, narratives about cultural identities and cultural politics. Migrant or mobile food, in the texts and cultural contexts discussed here, carries multiple significations of home. In other words, the transport and presentation of a variety of foods "are extremely complex and diversified expressions of place."[82] Often, in the new, diasporic context, the art of cooking has to be (re)learnt or the stories of particular foods retold. In representing or remembering a particular Indian food or meal being prepared, the pull of nostalgia is strong; yet the texts discussed here problematise the notion of a static, authentic dish/memory that can be recreated whole. Nostalgia makes way for adaptation and an acknowledgement that food is provisional, always on the move, and that recipes are not perfect. In *Afternoon Raag*, a friend tries to sniff out a recipe of the narrator's mother's; when she tries it for herself at home, however, "it was never, never right."[83] English "curry" evolved through adaptations using apple, various spices and dessicated coconut, though "where the idea originated of adding sultanas to the standard English works canteen curry is anybody's guess."[84]

Food, in Suleri's words, is a means "not simply of ordering a week or a day but of living inside history."[85] An influx of new foods from the global marketplace can be a threat to the types of memories rooted locally, but they also present the opportunity for the creation of different types of memories.[86] Perhaps ultimately, the "pleasures of the palate provid[e] more powerful bonds than knowledge" of different cultures.[87] Resource-fulness (the exaltation of the scrap or leftover), creativity, inventiveness, and mixing-it-all-up to taste are celebrated regardless of where a food has travelled from and where it is going to. The character of the old lady in the British television programme *The Kumars at No. 42* (2001), who can make anything from a small aubergine, is an affectionate jibe at the notion of homemade and at adaptability itself. The "real stuff" of how the world works is epitomised, as in Vikram Chandra's *Love and Longing in Bombay* (1997), in the very process of masala-grinding.[88]

---

[82] Marc Henri Piault, "Nourritures…?" *XI International Festival of Ethnographic Films Catalogue* (2002): 19.
[83] Chaudhuri, 82.
[84] Burton, 76.
[85] Suleri, 314.
[86] Sutton, 71.
[87] Narayan, 80.
[88] Vikram Chandra, *Love and Longing in Bombay* (London: Faber, 1997), 33.

Bibliography

Ali, Monica. *Brick Lane*. London: Doubleday, 2003.

—. "My Favourite Table." *Observer Food Magazine*, August 2003.

Argy, Stephanie. "Short Takes: A Loving Tribute to a Mother's Cooking." *American Cinematographer* (2002): 98.

Bakewell, Joan. Interview with Amrit and Rabindra KD Kaur Singh. *Belief*, Radio 3, December 27, 2002.

Banerji, Chitrita. "The Bengali Bonti." *Gastronomica: The Journal of Food and Culture* 1.2 (2001): 23-6.

Burton, David. *The Raj at Table: A Culinary History of the British in India*. London: Faber, 1993.

Candappa, Rohan. *Picklehead: From Ceylon to Suburbia; A Memoir of Food, Family and Finding Yourself*. London: Ebury Press, 2006.

Chandra, Vikram. *Love and Longing in Bombay*. London: Faber, 1997.

Chaudhuri, Amit. *Afternoon Raag*. London: Vintage, 1998.

Desai, Anita. *Fasting, Feasting*. London: Vintage, 1999.

England, Chris. *Balham to Bollywood*. London: Sceptre, 2002.

"50 Years Food and Drink: Food Summer Special." *The Guardian Weekend*, June 29, 2002.

Floyd, Janet and Laurel Forster. "Introduction: The Recipe in Its Cultural Contexts." In *The Recipe Reader: Narratives, Contexts, Traditions*. Ed. Janet Floyd and Laurel Forster. Aldershot: Ashgate, 2003. 1-14.

Fort, Matthew. "Eating Out." *The Guardian Weekend*, August 16, 2003. 73.

Freidberg, Susanne. "Not All Sweetness and Light: New Cultural Geographies of Food." *Social and Cultural Geography* 4.1 (2003): 3-6.

Ghosh, Amitav. "Nashawy." In *The Vintage Book of Indian Writing 1947-1997*. Ed. Salman Rushdie and Elizabeth West. London: Vintage, 1997. 409-21.

Hariharan, Githa. "The Remains of the Feast." In *The Vintage Book of Indian Writing 1947-1997*. Ed. Salman Rushdie and Elizabeth West,. London: Vintage, 1997. 422-9.

Jaffrey, Madhur. *Madhur Jaffrey's Indian Cookery*. London: BBC Books, 1982.

Kalra, Virinder. "The Political Economy of the Samosa." *South Asia Research* 24.1 (2004): 21-36

Kanga, Firdaus. "Trying to Grow." In *The Vintage Book of Indian Writing 1947-1997*. Ed. Salman Rushdie and Elizabeth West. London: Vintage, 1997. 326-55.

Kapranos, Alex. *Sound Bites: Eating on Tour with Franz Ferdinand.*
    London: Penguin, 2006.
Kaur Singh, Rabindra KD. *All Hands on Deck.* Twin Studio Collection,
    1997. http://www.singhtwins.co.uk/gal_page2.htm (accessed August
    25, 2006).
Kaur Singh, Amrit KD and Rabindra KD Kaur Singh. *Mr Singh's India.*
    Glasgow Gallery of Modern Art, 1999/2000.
    http://www.singhtwins.co.uk/ gals/public/singh.htm (accessed August
    25, 2006).
Manto, Saadat Hasan. "Toba Tek Singh." In *The Vintage Book of Indian
    Writing.* Ed. Salman Rushdie and Elizabeth West. London: Vintage,
    1997. 24-31.
Martens, Lydia, and Alan Warde. *Eating Out: Social Differentiation,
    Consumption and Pleasure.* Cambridge: Cambridge University Press,
    2000.
Melhuish, Clare. "The Cultural Imagery of Patel's *A Love Supreme.*" *The
    Architects' Journal* 2.9 (2001): 12.
Narayan, Uma. "Eating Cultures: Incorporation, Identity and Indian
    Food." *Social Identities* 1.1 (1995): 63-86.
Patel, Nilesh, dir. *A Love Supreme.* Les Beauchistes, 2001.
Piault, Marc Henri. "Nourritures…?" *XI International Festival of
    Ethnographic Films Catalogue,* 2002.
http://www.realindianfood.com (accessed April 5, 2007).
Roy, Arundhati. "Things Can Change in a Day." *Granta: India! The
    Golden Jubilee.* 57 (1997): 258.
Rushdie, Salman. "Introduction." In *The Vintage Book of Indian Writing
    1947-1997.* Ed. Salman Rushdie and Elizabeth West. London: Vintage,
    1997. ix-xxii.
Sardar, Ziauddin, and Borin Van Loon. *Introducing Cultural Studies.* New
    York: Totem Books, 1998.
Shamsie, Kamila. *Salt and Saffron.* London and New York: Bloomsbury,
    2000.
Sharma, Bulbul. *The Anger of Aubergines: Stories of Women and Food.*
    New Delhi: Kali for Women, 1997.
Sreedharan, Das. *The New Tastes of India.* London: Headline, 2001.
Suleri, Sara. "Meatless Days." In *The Vintage Book of Indian Writing
    1947-1997.* Ed. Salman Rushdie and Elizabeth West. London: Vintage,
    1997. 302-25.
Sutton, David. *Remembrance of Repasts: An Anthropology of Food and
    Memory.* Oxford: Berg, 2001.
Sweet, Matthew. *Inventing the Victorians.* London: Faber, 2001.

Van den Berghe, Pierre. "Ethnic Cuisine: Culture in Nature." *Ethnic and Racial Studies* 7.3 (1984): 387-97.

Varma, Pavan K. *Being Indian*. London: Arrow, 2006.

CHAPTER THREE

SWEET TASTE OF INDIA:
FOOD METAPHORS IN CONTEMPORARY
INDIAN FICTION IN ENGLISH

DANIELA ROGOBETE

Lingers on the tip of my tongue,
Gotta love the sweet taste of India.
Blame it on the beat of the drum,
God, I love the sweet taste of India.
(Aerosmith, "Taste of India")

"To eat is a behaviour that develops beyond its own ends, replacing, summing up and signalizing other behaviours [...] We might almost say that this 'polysemia' of food characterizes modernity."[1] Barthes's attempt to devise "a veritable grammar of food,"[2] and establish its centrality regarding other forms of social behaviour could be considered a starting point in a cultural and structuralist approach to food in relation to post/colonialism and national identity. Food—whether mixing and cooking its ingredients, eating and digesting it, assimilating or eliminating it—has been variously associated with life, survival, growth, death, love, sin, transience, memory and oblivion. It is because "food techniques" have been seen as "the repository of a whole experience, of the accumulated wisdom of our ancestors"[3] that different culinary practices have been associated with cultural stereotypes and used to remap national identity. The particular concern of the present discussion is with the particular relationship of food to cultural diversity and to processes of intermingling.

---

[1] Roland Barthes, *Mythologies* (New York: Hill and Wang, 1972), 25.
[2] Barthes, 22.
[3] Roland Barthes, "Towards a Psychology of Contemporary Food Consumption," in *Food and Culture: A Reader,* ed. Carolyn Counihan and Penny van Esterik (New York: Routledge, 1977), 24.

The tropic dimensions of food first appeared in colonial travel accounts and have reached their current form in postmodern, postcolonial and diasporic revaluations of national discourses and identities. The textualisation of food—and one excludes here those cookbooks that are no more than mere collections of recipes—permits an approach from a new perspective to such issues as negotiating social and cultural identities, accepting or rejecting the Other, and responding to cultural counter-colonisation and globalisation.

The problems of the terms *authenticity* and purity have preoccupied the postcolonial world which has tried to deconstruct them and expose the artificiality of such cultural constructs a long time before European poststructuralism attempted to destroy the hegemony of such concepts as authenticity, authorship and purity. The general attempt was to counterbalance Eurocentricity with new perspectives that might destroy the old dichotomy of the Western metropolitan authenticity and the native inauthenticity of the colonial reality, the latter to be authenticated only through metropolitan discourse. Authenticity is one of these concepts used and abused by multi-ethnic Indian society and its eclectic culture; culinary authenticity is also relativised through the multitude of regional varieties for the recipe of one single dish. This shows, once more, the Indian propensity towards hybridity and inclusiveness. Combined with an eagerness to demolish stereotypical descriptions it subtly creates spaces of cultural resistance. In fact, when associated with tastes and smells and analysed from this perspective, different types of food are able to remap territories, organise them according to olfactory criteria and distinguish among familiar, alien, threatening, sensual, spicy or dull spaces.

By turns showing its ability to function as a synecdoche for art and culture (Ashis Nandy), as a metonym for the Indian nation and as a metaphor for writing and creation, "food" seems to have earned its rightful place in Indian culture and society as a consequence of its special capacity to operate as a "social marker" (Arjun Appadurai) that regulates human relations and shapes the way in which whole cultural and spiritual territories may be recreated and remapped.

This essay attempts to theorise the ways in which food has a textualised and metaphorical presence in recent Indian writing in English. Such a theorisation will, I hope, enable the reopening of the debate about national and cultural identity and authenticity. The particular case of Indian food is complicated by the postcolonial, anthropological, political and social implications that inevitably arise. The tropes used in describing Indian regional foods consistently extend to aspects of social functions and features of hierarchic organisational, or they may permit subversive strategies and what might be characterized as culinary counter-colonialism. In every case such tropes appear to legitimise eclecticism and hybridity over limitation and purity. What Indian writers succeed in transmitting so subtly is a special emphasis upon a sense of community and belonging, upon family matters and human solidarity, all of which is conveyed predominantly through culinary metaphors. In such a literary context, it becomes as difficult to reach definite conclusions concerning "Indian authenticity," as it would be to speak about a unique, and authentic, Indian cuisine.

Writing Food, Digesting Stories

The South Asian space seems to place a peculiar focus on gastronomic matters and assign them highly symbolic dimensions and special social functions. Westernness, in its turn, has always taken a particular delight in the Asian wealth of spices and flavours, recipes and exotic concoctions. What we generally call "Indian cuisine" relies upon an ancient tradition going back 5000 years, a tradition authenticated by numerous archaeological findings in the valley of the Indus, including remains of preserved vegetables (cucumber and eggplant), cereals, herbs and medicinal plants. The rapid evolution in culinary tastes and practices based on tradition took various forms in different parts of the Indian subcontinent. Many of these distinctions are visible even today, emphasising the differences between North and South: Kashmiri and Mughal cuisines are still thought to preserve Chinese influences in the manner of the entire Northern part (using ghee, curd and cream), the Goan cuisine is considered to be influenced by the Portuguese whereas the Bengali and Assamese kitchens show the influence of East Asia and its culinary traditions.[4]

India seems to have always been a place that resists definite categorisations and strict dichotomies. If it is extremely difficult to find a precise location for authentic Indianness—in relation to culture, language, literature and national identity—it is equally difficult to define an authentic and unique *Indian cuisine.* Since authentic national identity in the Indian case might lie equally with the Hindus, the Muslims, Punjabis, Kashmiris or Parsis, so the identity of what we refer to as "Indian food" might as well be represented by Mughlai or Kashmiri, the Goan or Bengali, Tamil or Malayali cuisines, each of which may incorporate

---

[4] See Paul Fieldhouse, *Food and Nutrition: Customs and Culture* (Cheltenham: Nelson Thomas, 2002).

borrowings from other regional cuisines. Whether we refer to culture, identity or simply food, *authenticity* is a permanently challenged concept in India, one that is further blurred by postmodern eclecticism, the politics of the diaspora and globalization. The notion of the *authentic* appears to suggest everything that is appropriated by the mainstream as suggested in the Indians' favourite motto "take the best and leave the rest," a motto clearly divorced from purism and monologism. It could not be otherwise in a space where there are sixteen official languages and many more literatures and where "bread" itself can appear in a multitude of forms ranging from the Northern flat specialties *roti, paratha, bhatoora* to the yeasted *naan,* and the Southern *chapatti* to the *rotli* in Gujarat and *pulka* in Punjabi.

Theorists have tried to devise an entire "ethnography of food" starting from the coordinates of what is generally taken to be *the politics of food.* In the case of India, extreme culinary diversity and openness towards anything that might enrich its flavours can be equated to its cultural diversity and eclecticism. In an attempt to authenticate a national Indian cuisine, Ashis Nandy uses food as a synecdoche of culture, taking it to stand for

> a cultural marker of status, taste and cultivation but also [one that] carries the reflection of personal and collective milestones and traumata. It begins to mirror new constituents of self-definition.[5]

The mixture of gastronomic styles and influences indicates the Indian propensity towards diversity and plurality and its capacity of assimilating everything from religious beliefs and cultural practices to food.[1] The Indians were thus only too eager to assimilate the Greek saffron, the Chinese tea or the Portuguese and the British chilli, potato and cauliflower and the Arabian cinnamon. The Arabians were the first who apparently helped in increasing the interest in Indian spices by creating legends around them and weaving metaphorical correspondences that have finally led to the *textualisation of the culinary realm.*[6] As Shrabani Basu puts it:

> Spices, with their tingle and exoticism, brought a touch of colour and glamour to life in northern Europe which in the medieval period was lacking both. Spices helped preservation, disguised the bland from the

---

[5] Ashis Nandy, "The Changing Popular Culture of Indian Food: Preliminary Notes," *South Asia Research Journal* 24.1 (2004): 17.

[6] Parama Roy, "Reading Communities and Culinary Communities: The Gastropoetics of the South Indian Diaspora," *Positions* 10.2 (2002): 477.

rancid and brought a taste of oriental glamour into the bleak English winter.[7]

The abundance of Indian dishes, flavours, condiments and ingredients is usually used in descriptions of familiar meals or communitarian *wazas*[8] as a means of emphasising the inclination towards eclecticism and exquisite mélange, inclusiveness and hybridity. As a mixture of Asian and European cuisines, regional varieties and religious diets, the Indian cuisine is a denial of purism. The particular Indian interest in gastronomy corresponds to a long-standing tradition of textualising and metaphorising food which goes back to the old texts of Vedic and Sufi traditions, and continues in present-day literary productions.

Starting from the etymology of the word recipe (coming from the Latin *recipere* and defining a process of exchange), Susan Leonardi makes a connection between words and food that have to be ingested and digested in order to be understood. She refers to cooking as an operation whose result may be not only a "culinary text" but also a story/history on a metaphoric level since "like a story, a recipe needs a recommendation, a context, a point, a reason to be."[9] Churning ingredients equated with arranging words into literal or edible "coherence" becomes the recurrent metaphor in many Indian texts. In *Powers of Horror* Julia Kristeva has made the same connection between the actions of speaking and eating, as well as between words and food as the proper tools in the formation of subjectivity and definition of identity.[10] Kristeva, along with other theorists, has frequently emphasised the metaphoric value of food and the idea of its semiotic function as language mainly through synaesthesia and metonymy. Maud Ellmann goes even further to sustain that "eating is the origin of subjectivity"[11] whereas speech and writing can be seen as forms of fasting. As Gunew puts it:

> The fact that language issues from the same orifice in which nutrition is imbibed means that words and food are locked in eternal rivalry [...] Since

---

[7] Shrabani Basu, *Curry: The Story of the Nation's Favourite Dish* (Stroud, Gloucestershire: Sutton Publishing, 2003), 3.

[8] Traditional Indian feasts.

[9] Susan Leonardi, "Recipes for Reading: Summer Pastas, Lobster a la Riseholme, and Key Lime Pie," *PMLA* 104.3 (1989): 340.

[10] See Julia Kristeva, *Powers of Horror* (New York: Columbia University, 1982).

[11] Ellman qtd. in Sneja Gunew, "Mouthwork: Food and Language as the Corporeal Home for the Unhoused Diasporic Body in South Asian Women's Writing," *Journal of Commonwealth Literature* 40.2 (2005): 98.

language must compete with food to gain sole possession of the mouth, we must either speak or go hungry, or shut up and eat.[12]

No discussion of the textualisation of food can ignore the production of cookbooks which, along with food metaphors, may offer delimitations of national identity, as Arjun Appadurai has argued. Cookbooks provide particular forms of textualisation and provide "culinary maps," combinations of gastronomic discourses and national narratives meant to counter biased descriptions and imperial discourses. Initially transmitted orally, and thereby handed down from one generation to another, Indian recipes were first recorded and gathered, especially during the colonial period, by foreigners eager to impress their mother country with exotic dishes. From their origins as part of the collections of Anglo-Indian women, recipes have evolved into complex texts combining autobiographical anecdotes and culinary explanations, national discourses and historical accounts. The traditional eighteenth-century cookery book has gradually become a "gastronomic literary text" relying—according to Steve Jones and Ben Taylor in "Food Writing and Food Cultures"—upon rules of etiquette and practice, upon dietetic recommendations, spicy stories and evocations of other earlier gastronomic episodes.[13] Madhur Jaffrey's cookbooks *A Taste of India* and *Invitation to Indian Cooking* or Shrabani Basu's *Curry: The Story of the Nation's Favourite Dish* are generally cited as the "best sellers" of Indian cuisine, and even as significant "gastro-autobiographical endeavours"[14] of cookery writing. These cookbooks combine recipes and culinary instructions with meandering stories of spices, dishes and exquisite delicatessens that almost transform them into Indian gastronomic epics. The traditional restriction of professional cookery to men and domestic cookery to women was challenged when cookery (envisaged as *haute cuisine*) was detached from the realm of domesticity and acquired new dimensions that offered women alternative forms of self-expression.

In the case of India authenticity and legitimacy have thus become very confusing matters as a consequence of the impossibility to authenticate a unique national culture and literature, let alone a unique national cuisine. Arjun Appadurai argues that it was only after India's independence in 1947 that the multiplicity of recipes was gathered into a national cuisine though it never relied upon a unique Indian taste but upon a huge diversity

---

[12] Gunew, 98.
[13] Steve Jones and Ben Taylor, "Food Writing and Food Cultures: The Cases of Elizabeth David and Jane Grigson, *Cultural Studies 4.2* (2001): 171-88.
[14] Roy, 484.

of culinary practices.[15] In his comments on Hindu gastro-politics Appadurai highlights the social function and moral meaning of food together with its semiotic functions of homogenizing and heterogenizing groups of people in terms of caste affiliation, gender and hierarchic distinctions and commensality, placing it between "metonymic hazard and metaphoric convenience."[16]

By coining the term "gastro-politics" to describe everything that is related to "social transactions around food,"[17] Appadurai thus presents an analysis of food establishing three major domains where it might be revealed as a semiotic instrument: in households where food becomes a social as well as domestic currency, with its symbolic hierarchic organisation that assign people different roles according to gender, age and kinship, in temples, where it becomes sacred and acquires particular dimensions in the joined act of worshipping and offering, and in huge gatherings such as weddings and *wazas* where the act of hosting highlights the vital importance of commensality.[18] Commensality, comprising "rituals of nation-making,"[19] has been regarded as a way of reinforcing human bonding and a sense of communality and solidarity, sometimes acquiring political and social significances. Hindu and Vedic traditions are governed by the idea of offering food as a gift to the gods in order to gain their benevolence; accordingly, "a guest is a gift of God" and should be lavishly attended upon.

Appadurai refers to food as a social marker able to build social relations and define group or individual identity. It can be a provider of homogeneity when it functions as a sign of equality, intimacy and solidarity among people and one of heterogeneity when it emphasises rank, distance and social segmentation. As Arjun Appadurai writes:

> In a cultural universe that sets considerable store by a host of heterogeneous persons, groups, forces, and powers, food (whether "hot" or "cold," raw or cooked, sacred or sullied) always raises the possibility of homogenizing the actors linked by it, whether they are husband and wife, servant or master, worshiper or deity. [...] This is achieved by a variety of rules which regulate contact with food, prohibit certain classes of food to

---

[15] See Arjun Appadurai, "How to Make a National Cuisine: Cookbooks in Contemporary India," *Comparative Studies in Society and History* 30.1 (1988): 3-24.
[16] Arjun Appadurai, "Gastro-Politics in Hindu South Asia," *American Ethnologist* 8.3 (1981): 507.
[17] Appadurai, "Gastro-Politics in Hindu South Asia," 495.
[18] Appadurai, "Gastro-Politics in Hindu South Asia," 497-508.
[19] Roy, 484.

certain classes of persons, restrict certain foods to certain contexts, dictate sequences of serving and eating, allocate distinct roles to different individuals in the cooking, serving, and eating cycle, and so on. Of course, the cultural notion that food has an inherently homogenizing capacity (by virtue of its transformability into blood and semen) is itself converted from a metonymic hazard to a metaphoric convenience in the contexts where sharing, equality, solidarity, and community are, within limits, perceived as desirable results.[20]

Food as Creator of Spaces

Besides its unanimously recognised part in shaping social relations and defining identities, food can also operate as a creator of spaces in the general process of remapping cultural territories. In postcolonial texts references to Indian spices, descriptions of traditional meals and different culinary rituals, and the use of Indian names for more or less untranslatable traditional dishes have been generally used as strategies seeking to subvert the metropolitan discourse. These apparently insignificant matters created the opportunity to resist cultural erasure and to engender spaces of resistance. Charming the coloniser with a square, delicious meal could become a good way of winning him over, weakening his power and strengthening the position of the subaltern. The early European embrace of Indian cuisine has been deemed to be an attempt to tame the wild by adopting, adjusting and sometimes translating its culinary tastes. The opposite movement was a contestation of the imperial discourse through domesticity impregnated by Indian nationalistic presentations of home and household. Bhabha's "ambivalence of mimicry" can be said to function in this case too, through culinary appropriation and transformation. Theory has placed colonial discourse between mimesis and mimicry in an attempt to warn against the dangers of double vision and partial representations of otherness. For Bhabha *mimicry* represents a metonymy of presence, "a sign of a double articulation,"[21] an erratic, eccentric strategy of authority related to the play between difference and desire. The coloniser's desire of both understanding and subjecting the Other makes him mimic the native's discourse only to better impose the metropolitan one. To the same extent the native can mimic the metropolitan discourse with the intention to

---

[20] Appadurai, "Gastro-Politics in Hindu South Asia," 507.
[21] Homi Bhabha, "On Mimicry and Man: The Ambivalence of Colonial Discourse," in *Modern Literary Theory,* ed. Philip Rice and Paul Waugh (London: Routledge, 1989), 235.

appropriate the "vocabularies of power" and make them work in his favour as a weapon of passive resistance. The same may happen when the Other's culinary habits and practices are mimicked and appropriated so that subjection might acquire insidious forms. The result, in fact, is highly ambivalent according to Bhabha since enjoying and eating somebody else's food does not necessarily means "consuming" the Other but sometimes letting oneself be engulfed by Otherness. Indian eclecticism has also operated in the gastronomic field by assimilating some of the coloniser's culinary habits while at the same time seducing him with indigenous traditional food:

> Far from being a culturally pure enclave of Britishness in the empire, the Anglo-Indian kitchen was a site of cultural interactions and interchange. The voracious appetite of the British Empire was nourished not just by the roast beef of old England, but also by the chutney and curry of India.[22]

In postcolonial terms food can participate in the process of mapping out cultural identities and represents one of the means of simultaneously generating self-understanding and acceptance of the Other by understanding his food and culinary habits and by recurring to what Uma Narayan calls "democracy of the palate."[23] The cultural stereotypes and biased descriptions perpetuated by the earliest colonial travel accounts— mainly interested in stressing exoticism and remoteness, and either eulogising Indian spirituality and beauty or vilifying its dirtiness and excessive sensuality—and the perpetual oscillation between the wholehearted embrace of Indianness and its rejection find their equivalents in similar acts of embracing or rejecting "Indian food." Even if criticised for its powerful flavours and strange combinations of ingredients, Indian regional dishes, once brought to Europe, have enjoyed a tremendous success. Food was deemed to provide a special strategy of counteracting historical and political forces with a particular form of "food counter-colonialism." To European colonialism, India responded with a culinary form of imperialism. Uma Narayan suggests that colonising and understanding India, ingesting it into the Empire, also meant "eating India" whereby imperial violence and eagerness for the subjection and erasure of the Other was translated by means of a cannibalistic metaphor

---

[22] Mary Procida, "Feeding the Imperial Appetite: Imperial Knowledge and Anglo-Indian Domesticity," *Journal of Women's History* 15.2 (2003): 143.
[23] See Uma Narayan, "Eating Cultures: Incorporation, Identity and Indian Food," *Social Identities* 1.1 (1995): 63-86.

into an act of eating.[24] Far from being a defeat, this process was paradoxically the very thing that ensured the survival of traditional dishes and culinary practices, a process that amounts to cultural survival.

Since there is no unique Indian cuisine and it is impossible to locate authentic Indianness, the attempt to determine what "Indian food" might represent for a Westerner leads to a composite image made up of representative items taken from different Indian ethnic cuisines. If Barthes makes steak and chips emblems of French identity, then spices might be taken as the very essence of Indian cuisine, almost synonymous with Indianness. Metaphorically the migration of spices and their arrival in India at different times, occasioned by different invasions, hints at the consequent migration of ideas, concepts and cultural practices. Tracing the migration of food and the various regional cooking traditions sometimes means writing a narrative of the national-diasporic identity and devising a map where national and geographical delimitations are based upon culinary tastes and practices.

Once considered a means of distinguishing between colonisers and colonised within the South Asian space, various Indian regional dishes have succeeded in blurring political, social and racial boundaries indicating once more what Appadurai established as the homogenizing function of food.[25] The extensive migration of Indian specialities makes it difficult today, especially for a non-Asian person, to disentangle the many culinary borrowings, influences, assimilations and displacements. The problem of "authenticity" recurs when theorists argue that displacing dishes from their original location and taking them into an alien environment, even commodifying and turning what used to be home-made into "fast food," makes it impossible to authenticate a specific dish. The concept of "authentic flavour" is consequently lost or turned into a global "common property." An example of this fact is that nobody, in Ashis Nandy's opinion, remembers today that "snacks" originate in the Indian *tiffin*, now turned into another metaphor of gastronomic diversity pertaining to no particular cultural space.[26]

Regional varieties of food may also create, beyond the ethnic delimitations that they suggest, sensual spaces where flavours and fragrances distinguish among different territories governed by particular dishes and culinary tastes. The alchemic concoctions of spices and vegetables, and the intoxicating combinations of flavours, may engender

---

[24] Elspeth Probyn, "Beyond Food/Sex: Eating and the Ethics of Existence," *Theory, Culture and Society* 16.2 (1999): 21.
[25] Appadurai, "Gastro-Politics in Hindu South Asia," 494.
[26] Nandy, 13.

spaces of love and hate, loss and forgiveness, sensuality and passion according to the unwritten laws of the senses. By extensively alluding to spices and flavours most Indian texts create olfactory maps of sensual spaces that bear resemblance to what Paul Rodaway theorised as *smellscapes* in his essay "Sensuous Geographies." It is because "smell can be spatially ordered and place-related" that this olfactory geography is able to generate a strong connection between individuals and their environments. In so doing, it redefines Indianness from metaphoric perspectives and renders familiar the distant spaces where the Indian spirit emerges. To quote Rodaway:

> Olfactive geographies are not merely "smell maps" or even "smellscapes," but complex emotional encounters with discrete olfactory events, odours passing through time as well as space. Immediate olfactory encounters are perhaps quite a discontinuous geography, but the rich evocations of remembered smellscapes suggest that underlying this is a more continuous and synthetic olfactory geography.[27]

This sensual delimitation of space works for India too, where is often emphasised. Speaking about the intimate relation between smell and the exotic offer a vivid description of the encounter with the Indian space which can be best understood and appropriated through a complete opening of the senses:

> No account of India, from Kipling to recent popular novels, […] fails to evoke the peculiar smell of that subcontinent, half corrupt, half aromatic, a mixture of dung, sweat, heat, dust, rotting vegetation and spices. [28]

The same spatial attributes of food can become obvious when mnemonic dimensions are activated. What is activated along with them is the capacity to recreate familiar spaces and entire homelands through sensory and emotional functions. This particular dimension of food particularly emphasised in diasporic writings, brings out aspects related to the problems of acceptance abroad, preservation of national identity and resistance to "cultural colonisation." Food, flavours and the mechanism of Proustian involuntary memory succeed in recreating India's magic taste and a sense of closeness and belonging.

---

[27] Paul Rodaway, "Sensuous Geographies," *Cultural Geography: Critical Concepts in the Social Sciences,* ed. Nigel Thrift and Sarah Whatmore (London: Routledge, 2004), 78.

[28] Porteous qtd. in Rodaway, 81.

When Metaphors Spice up the Food

This section seeks to illustrate the theoretical points established so far. The examples come from contemporary Indian texts written in English that make use of food and culinary metaphors as means of illustrating problems related to hybridity and eclecticism. Metaphorising food has a very long tradition on the Indian subcontinent. The "spice of speech" of the Sufi tradition, referring to metaphor and alluding to the "kernel of knowledge" hidden in any human soul and waiting to be revealed, and the Indian propensity towards metaphorisation have become recurrent images in Indian contemporary texts. The metaphor of the artist as a master of mixing ingredients and its application to the practice of writing has a long tradition and has been continuously diversified. Many Indian authors residing in India, but especially those living abroad and writing in English, tend to rely on the metaphoric meanings of food in order to emphasise the diversity of readings that such a topic might engender: national and nationalistic, geo-political and cultural or gendered interpretations based on family and domestic readings.

As a sign of this, different writers and theorists metaphorically equate Indianness, as conveyed by food, with various traditional products: spices as the essence of Indianness (Rushdie, Kunzru), samosa as a metonym for Indianness in England (Virinder Kalra), curry or chapatti (Desai, Ghosh), pickles (Rushdie, Arundhati Roy). In so doing they establish a genuine gastronomic map of India as shown in Kiran Desai's recent novel *The Inheritance of Loss*:

> She liked to keep him company in the kitchen as he told her stories. He gave her bits of dough to roll into *chapatis* and showed her how to make them perfectly round, but hers came out in all kinds of shapes. "Map of India," he would say, dismissing one.[29]

The notion of Indianness becomes a cultural construct in Anita Desai's fiction. Intermingled voices and metaphoric expressions aim to reveal the Indian Westernised "cosmopolis" located somewhere between the seductive metropolis and the traditional "polis" where confused inhabitants struggle to redefine their identity. References to traditional dishes and spices are introduced in her novels as means of recreating the broken bond with the flavour and taste of the past and its values. Authors such as Narayan, Bharati Mukherjee, Hari Kunzru and Amitav Ghosh use culinary allusions in order to represent the cultural shock on a smaller

---

[29] Kiran Desai, *The Inheritance of Loss* (London: Penguin Books, 2006), 56.

scale by translating it into the clash between the dietary differences experienced by an Indian in the West. The Indian gastronomic lavishness and indulgence in flavours and tastes are confronted with the frugal snacks, the packaged food and greasy fast-food products of the West; this clash between two totally different gastronomic traditions stands for the migrant's disillusionment with the West.

Examples of this kind abound in Indian texts. In the last section of Anita Desai's *Fasting, Feasting* America is rejected by the young protagonist who refuses to adopt what he considers to be the American unhealthy culinary habits and continuously wonders "what is the more dangerous in this country, the pursuit of health or of sickness."[30] The protagonist in Bharati Mukherjee's *Wife* finds it extremely difficult to adjust to a Western style of life presented in a stark contrast with her glamorous expectations. Coming to terms with the experience of immigration signifies for Dimple Dasgupta assimilating strange habits and pretending she can cope with a harsh reality; in this foreign reality in which she seems to be sleepwalking even going to the supermarket and buying Western food can be an alien experience where one can get trapped forever:

> She had expected pain when she had come to America, had told herself that pain was part of any new beginning [...] but she had not expected her mind to be strained like this, beyond endurance. She had not anticipated inertia, exhaustion, endless indecisiveness. If, in those early days in Queens, the man selling cheesecake had not trapped her, she might have been free, even reckless.[31]

Another example related to the same clash of cultures translated into culinary terms occurs in Kiran Desai's *The Inheritance of Loss* where regional identity is defined by its gastronomic dimensions:

> "Everyone knows," said the cook. "Coastal people eat fish and see how much cleverer they are, Bengalis, Malayalis, Tamils. Inland they eat too much grain, and it slows the digestion—especially millet—forms a big heavy ball. The blood goes to the stomach and not to the head. Nepalis make good soldiers, coolies, but they are not so bright at their studies. Not their fault, poor things."[32]

---

[30] Anita Desai, *Fasting, Feasting* (London: Vintage, 2000), 205.
[31] Bharati Mukherjee, *Wife* (New York: Fawcett Crest, 1975), 115.
[32] Kiran Desai, 73.

The care with which authors write about food and its assimilation, suggests a variety of meanings ranging from warm communality to the attempt to keep tradition alive, and gives a sensual inventory of the multitude of culinary traditions in India. Distinguishing among dishes and flavours means delimitating spaces and defining identities.

> She sent for Kashmiri food, of course, but also for the tandoori and Mughlai cuisines of north India, the boti kababs, the murgh makhani, and for the fish dishes of the Malabar coast, for the marsala dosas of Madras and the fabled early pumpkins of the coast of Coromandel, for the hot pickle curries of Hyderabad, for kulfi and barfi and pista-ki-lauz, and for sweet Bengali sandesh. Her appetite had grown to subcontinental size. It crossed all frontiers of language and custom. She was vegetarian and nonvegetarian, fish- and meat-eating, Hindu, Christian and Muslim, a democratic, secularist omnivore.[33]

Relations with the metropolis are equally shaped by what is eaten, how it is cooked and, surprisingly, how it is pronounced:

> 8:00: the cook saved his reputation, cooked a chicken, brought it forth, proclaiming it "roast bastard," just as in the Englishman's favourite joke book of natives using incorrect English. But sometimes, eating that roast bustard, the judge felt the joke might also be on him, and he called for another rum, took a big gulp, and kept eating, feeling as if he were eating himself, since he, too, was (was he?) part of the fun.[34]

Cooking one's own traditional meal, spicing everything with the right flavours, and struggling to find the proper ingredients, all can be seen as attempts to recreate the familiar space by recreating its tastes and smells. Cooking becomes a weapon of revenge for Hind, a character in Salman Rushdie's *The Satanic Verses* whose dissatisfaction with the metropolis makes her strike back by recreating her homelands through the dishes she prepares: "People came from all over London to eat her samosas, her Bombay chaat, her gulab jamans straight from Paradise [...] She was the mistress now. Victory!"[35]

Amitav Ghosh's references to food—though sparse—offer subtle re-enactments of the "invisible bonds linking people to one another through

---

[33] Salman Rushdie, *Shalimar the Clown* (London: Jonathan Cape, 2005), 202.
[34] Desai, 62-3.
[35] Salman Rushdie, *The Satanic Verses* (London: Vintage, 2000), 248-9.

personifications of their commonality."[36] In Ghosh's world, which is one tormented by war, grief and loss, by the constant clash between tradition and modernity, and by the ironically intricate workings of history, the rare allusions to dishes and meals recreate or reinforce family ties and a sense of communality. Whether alluding to meagre snacks or lavish meals abounding in traditional specialties and exquisite flavours, Ghosh reconstructs the specificity of a particular space, drawing subtle yet undeniable boundaries between spaces, identities and cultures. In Ghosh's fiction food becomes synonymous with traditional order and family happiness in the same way in which "kitchen" is synecdochically equated to "home." It can suggest communion and solidarity, and sometimes it provides subversive strategies of fighting the Empire as in the case of the inoffensive chapatti turned, in *The Glass Palace,* into a political weapon:

> Chapattis—those most unremarkable of everyday foods—had begun to circulate from village to village, as though in warning. No one knew where they came from or who had put them in motion—but somehow people had known that a great convulsion was on its way.[37]

By referring to food and dietary habits, Ghosh succeeds in drawing a vivid picture of inter-ethnic relations and racial, colonial and social hierarchies, cultural delimitations and taboo-breaking. The fear of racial contamination by food becomes the fear of turning into the Other if eating his food and is ironically sanctioned by Ghosh: "A chapatti won't turn you into a savage, you know."[38] Such episodes provide ironic comments upon the absurdity of racial prejudices and colonial claims, giving concepts such as duty, freedom, civilisation, an ambiguous turn. Colonial stereotypical dichotomies and a distorted sense of duty (materialised in the blind passivity of letting oneself be engulfed by the Empire while at the same time unconditionally ingesting it) are frequently denounced and ridiculed:

> Every meal at the officers' mess [...] was an adventure, a glorious infringement of taboos. They ate foods that none of them had ever touched at home: bacon, ham and sausages at breakfast; roast beef and pork chops for dinner. They drank whiskey, beer and wine. Smoked cigars, cigarettes and cigarillos. Nor was this just a matter of satisfying appetites: every mouthful had a meaning—each represented an advance towards the

---

[36] Amitav Ghosh, *The Glass Palace* (London: Harper Collins Publishers, 2001), 47.
[37] Ghosh, 246.
[38] Ghosh, 415.

evolution of a new, more complete kind of Indian. All of them had stories to tell about how their stomachs had turned the first time they had chewed upon a piece of beef or pork. [...] Yet they had persisted, for there were small but essential battles and they tested not just their manhood, but also their fitness to enter the class of officers. They had to prove, to themselves as well as to their superiors, that they were eligible to be rulers, to qualify as members of an elite: that they had vision enough to rise above the ties of their soil, to overcome the responses instilled in them by their upbringing.[39]

It seems to be something recurrent for Indian writers to use the "magic taste of India" and deconstruct it to its smallest elements to be translated into evocative images and dizzy combinations of conflicting flavours. In Salman Rushdie's novels combining spices and ingredients becomes an occasion of giving free vent to imagination and mixing together bizarre characters and miraculous events, surrealist elements and grotesque images to emphasise the values of pluralism and heterogeneity and to disrupt any sense of normality and pre-established order. He addresses all the senses in a whirl of tastes, smells and sights which alters reality and casts a spell upon the reader. In this he relies upon taking pleasure not only in the taste of a particular dish but in its flavour, appearance, texture and combination of colours, transforming in this way the pleasure of eating into an aesthetic pleasure. Cooking and eating thus become metaphors for any artistic endeavour. As the works of Salman Rushdie show, the intermingling of stories and lives, digressions and loose ends transforms the writer into a chef in perfect control of the art of pickles and chutney making and the reader into a "swallower of lives"—another metaphor coming from the culinary lexical field ("To understand a life you have to swallow a world").

To pickle is to give immortality, after all; fish, vegetables, fruit hang embalmed in spice-and-vinegar; a certain alteration, a slight intensification of taste, is a small matter, surely? The art is to change the flavour in degree, but not in kind; and above all (in my thirty jars and a jar) to give it shape and form—that is to say, meaning. (I have mentioned my fear of absurdity).

One day, perhaps, the world may taste the pickles of history. They may be too strong for some palates, their smell may be overpowering, tears may rise to eyes; I hope nevertheless that it will be possible to say of them that

---

[39] Ghosh, 278-9.

they possess the authentic taste of truth [...] that they are, despite
everything, acts of love.[40]

With Rushdie cooking, pickling and chutney making in *Midnight's
Children*, the combinations of spices in *The Moor's Last Sigh*, the
extravagant feasts and culinary excesses of *Shalimar the Clown*, suggest
the way in which the Rushdiean narration is built by putting together
disparate items, stirring them by means of shocking images and
intertextual associations till they form a coherent whole and their flavours
combine. Cooking becomes synonymous with a secret, sensual alchemy
meant to achieve the perfect taste and on a symbolic level, to help
extracting the truth. Pickling is one of the central metaphors in *Midnight's
Children* that suggests the extraction of "the authentic taste of truth"
which increases the acidity of a witty, spontaneous narration, and winds in
apparently never-ending loops. Pickling becomes synonymous with
writing, both seen as acts of preservation of the past and of its truths. The
repetitive use of some stylistic devices, the juxtaposition of apparently
disconnected elements, and the multiplication of approaches (standing for
diverse ingredients) may ensure the authenticity of the taste of truth and
may provide a subtle weapon against the fixity of thought which Rushdie
so much criticises. Pickles and writing govern the fictional universe in
Midnight's Children where story-telling is turned into another instance of
digesting lives and stories, of fragments of family or collective history, all
operating according to "dietary laws" which assist in achieving the perfect
chutney, the proper mixture of memories, dreams, ideas and fragrances.
The chutneyfication of history implies a particular approach to history,
which is seen as a palimpsestic narrative juxtaposing layers of recorded
facts, fiction, re-imagined events, distorted official recordings and fantasy.

Starting from Rushdie's metaphor of the "chutneyfication of history"
in *Midnight's Children,* Mita Banerjee turns chutney into the perfect
cultural metaphor situated at the intersection of postmodernism and
postcolonialism. She finds common points in the treatment of *chutney* in
the novels of Salman Rushdie, Michael Ondaatje and Bharati Mukherjee.
She further equates chutney with a palimpsest lacking a strict hierarchy
among its layers but never losing sight of the major ingredients: "Thus the
chutney itself is symbolic of an intricate web of relations where layers can
no longer be re-hierarchized and interpenetrate; where each detail,
however tiny, will affect the taste of the whole, where every mustard seed

---

[40] Salman Rushdie, *Midnight's Children* (London: Vintage, 1995), 444.

makes a difference."[41] These features make the chutney better suited to translate cultural syncretism, hybridity and heterogeneity, intertextuality and interculturality, as well as the migrant experiences and that of story telling. The identification established between culinary and narrative chutneys transforms chutney into a metaphor for the interconnectedness established between (his-) stories, spaces and people together with events, realities and selves, leaking one into the other.

The culinary metaphors so frequent in Rushdie's fiction stand for an aesthetic creed and convey the idea of mixture, relativisation and ambiguity. The result is a spicy little bit of everything where the proportion of truth and magic cannot be properly determined. Rushdie shares with Arundhati Roy an interest in pickles and preserves as a metaphorical way of suggesting the difficult process of gathering facts and stories, blending them not with vinegar but with irony, humour and scepticism in order to extract the truth. Roy uses her pickles as a way of preserving the conflicting versions of history in order to obtain the right taste and flavour, to go beyond familial dissentions, socio-political ideologies and caste prejudices. Rushdie's "chutneyfication of history" and Arundhati Roy's "pickling" of alternative histories become a culinary measuring of history. This is also the case with Sara Suleri. In her *Meatless Days* Suleri discusses the metaphoric significance of food and "all the transmogrifications of which it is capable"[42] by suggesting that gastrophilic histories should be constructed as alternative histories in order to counteract the major narratives:

> Food certainly gave us a way not simply of ordering a week or a day but of living inside history, measuring everything we remembered against a chronology of cooks. Just as Papa had his own yardstick with which to measure history and would talk about the Ayub era, or the second martial law, or the Bhutto regime, so my sisters and I would place ourselves in time by remembering and naming cooks.[43]

Recording history becomes not only a matter of taste but also a question of smell and intuition. Smells and fragrances associated with dishes and spices play such an important part in Indian novels that this power of smell becomes in Salman Rushdie's *Midnight's Children* one of Saleem's magical gifts permitting him to feel the approach of future

---

[41] Mita Banerjee, *Chutneyfication of History: Salman Rushdie, Michael Ondaatje, Bharati Mukherjee and the Postcolonial Debate* (Heidelberg: C. Winter, 2002), 99.
[42] Sara Suleri, *Meatless Days* (Chicago: University of Chicago Press, 1989), 34.
[43] Suleri, 34.

disasters. Upon losing his telepathic gifts and being no longer able to hear the pulse of the world he gains the ability to smell it. Saleem's enormous nose—alluding to the Indian god Ganesh, son of Shiva and Parvati, the "elephant-headed," "mammoth-trunked [...] garrulous" god who is said to have played an important part in the writing of the Mahabharata—becomes "the place where the outside world meets the world inside you."[44] Rushdie develops an entire science of "nasal ethics" where synaesthetic metaphors find their best expression. Odours and fragrances play an important part in *Midnight's Children* where they occasion unexpected associations of words and images: among so many disturbing smells "perfumes of emotions," "fragrance of the past,"[45] of the present, and of different people, symbolised here by Tai Bibi, the oldest whore on Earth able to imitate everybody's smell. Saleem makes a classification of odours by colours:

> Early attempts at ordering: I tried to classify smells by colour—boiling underwear and the printer's ink of the Daily Jang, shared a quality of blueness, while old teak and fresh farts were both dark brown. Motor-cars and graveyards I jointly classified as grey [...] there was, too, classification-by-weight: flyweight smells (paper), bantam odours (soap-fresh bodies, grass, perspiration, queen-of-the-night); shaki-korma and bicycle-oil were light-heavy-weight in my system, while anger, patchouli, treachery and dung were among the heavyweight stinks of the earth. And I had a geometric system also: the roundness of joy and the angularity of ambition; I had elliptical smells, and also ovals and squares [...] a lexicographer of the nose, I travelled Bunder Road and the P.E.C.H.S.; a lepidopterist, I snared whiffs like butterflies in the net of my nasal hairs. [...] Having realised the crucial nature of morality, having sniffed out the smells could be sacred or profane, I invented in the isolation of my scooter-trips, the science of nasal ethics.[46]

In the case of an author such as Hari Kunzru, smell and odours are treated as means of delimitating between cultural spaces. The hero of his novel *The Impressionist* is in a permanent search for identity and ends up by taking up a multitude of personae, desperately trying to achieve the perfect Englishness and civility even if this means hiding his Indianness under successive layers of lies and deception.

---

[44] Rushdie, *Midnight's Children*, 17.
[45] Rushdie, *Midnight's Children*, 317.
[46] Rushdie, *Midnight's Children*, 318.

Most of the time Bobby is free to reinvent himself, slipping into a new identity [...] His pretences are flimsy at first and he soon learns that looks and accent are not enough. There is for example the question of smell. Like everyone Bobby has always wondered about the grim English war against cookery, their inexplicable liking for tasteless slabs of meat, unspiced vegetables and sweetened concoctions of flour and fat.[47]

Relying upon his Indian instinctive inclination towards odours, he tries to locate the essence of national identity in smell, thus undergoing a complex search for the English smell but what he discovers is "rancid butter. With perhaps a hint of raw beef. The underlying wift of Empire."[48]

The Indian diet has always oscillated between abundance and scarcity. The fear of starvation generates impressive images as shown in the hunger-inspired dreams in Kunzru's novel. His main character dreams of "a land mad of stacked chapattis and curds, populated by vegetable girls with okra fingers and aubergine breasts and saucy looks in their green-pea eyes."[49] His insatiable appetite matches his eagerness in adopting as many identities as convenient and digesting as many lives and stories as possible. With other authors this fear of starvation develops into a real obsession reaching alarming degrees of concern as in Hanif Kureishi's *My Ear at His Heart*:

As children, father wanted us to eat, of course. How many family dramas are situated around what children will, and will not, put into their bodies? [...] The "starving of India" seemed to be on TV a lot when I was a child. I guess were looking at the first of many televised famines.[50]

The literary counterpart of this food obsession occurs in elaborate descriptions of feasts, and in sensual displays of fragrances, recipes and mixtures of condiments.

In Anita Desai's *Cry, the Peacock* and Bharati Mukerjee's *Wife* cooking becomes a way of expressing oneself, a means of asserting one's will especially for women while confinement into one's kitchen, finding one's place among pots and spices, may sometimes appear as a means of imprisoning female characters in a traditional world of domesticity. This strategy is often used as an alternative voice they find in order to assert their strength. Along with weaving and singing, dancing or telling stories,

---

[47] Hari Kunzru, *The Impressionist* (London: Penguin Books, 2002), 249.

[48] Kunzru, 250.

[49] Kunzru, 59.

[50] Hanif Kureishi, *My Ear at His Heart: Reading My Father* (London: Faber & Faber, 2004), 59.

cooking often becomes a subversive way of undermining the patriarchal discourse.

The metaphoric treatment of food recurrent in Indian texts is extended to the representations of eating disorders. They often reveal problems of self-awareness, self-esteem, cultural and national identity and quite often, lack of adaptation to a hostile reality. Many of these disorders are related to socio-political afflictions of inability to become integrated into a community, or the eagerness to gain acceptance in a new environment. Rejecting Indian food is sometimes equal to rejecting tradition and striving to embrace a new identity. Desai's *Fasting, Feasting* deals with a cultural clash translated into food assimilation; sent to America to study, Arun, the son of a middleclass Indian family exercises his "resistance to being included"[51] by obstinately refusing to adopt the American diet and by analysing its devastating effects upon the family where he lives. The mother, a fierce shopaholic, suffers from bulimia and the daughter from anorexia, a sign of "outrage against neglect, against misunderstanding, against inattention to her unique and singular being and its hungers."[52]

Salman Rushdie provides another example of eating disorder taken to stand for loss of identity and self-esteem. Boony, the beautiful Kashmiri dancer in *Shalimar the Clown*, leaves her husband and becomes the mistress of the American Ambassador to India. Far from conquering the world and broadening her horizons, she finds herself confined within the world of an apartment, reduced to a pretty body available at any moment. The burden of losing her family, her friends and ultimately her identity makes her start eating excessively. This is a desperate attempt to bring back Kashmir, now represented only by the sweets and flavours of its cuisine:

> But her narcotic of choice turned out to be food. At a certain point early in the second year of her captivity, she began, with great seriousness and a capacity for excess learned from the devil-city itself, to eat. If her world would not expand, her body could. She took to gluttony with the same bottomless enthusiasm she had once for sex, diverting the immense force of her erotic requirements from her bed to her table.[53]

Only when Boony comes home, though despised and thought dead, can she get rid of the immense burden of the absent Kashmir in her soul that made her seek it in its food. The coming to terms with her fate, her

---

[51] Anita Desai, *Fasting, Feasting*, 171.

[52] Anita Desai, *Fasting, Feasting*, 214.

[53] Salman Rushdie, *Shalimar the Clown*, 201.

rejection by the community, which has transformed her into a living ghost, helps her to regain the beautiful shapes she once had as the most graceful dancer in Kashmir. Her rehabilitation coincides with the strengthening of her body:

> This third-phase Boony was beautiful in a new way, the bruised, life-hardened, imperfect way of an adult woman. It was her reason that had been bruised most deeply and at night those bruises still hurt.[54]

Excessive eating regarded as an attempt to revive India and its impressive inclusiveness is illustrated by another episode, this time taken from *The Satanic Verses,* where "pluralistic openness of the mind" is matched by a similar "parallel eclecticism" in the kitchen:

> Gradually her espousal of the cause of gastronomic pluralism grew into a grand passion. [...] As she devoured the highly spiced dishes of Hyderabad and the high-faluting yoghurt sauces of Lucknow her body began to alter, because all that food had to find a home somewhere, and she began to resemble the wide rolling land mass itself, the subcontinent without frontiers, because food passes across any boundary you care to mention.[55]

In the era when globalisation afflicts economies and policies, spaces and identities, food is not able to escape it either. Commodification and mass production tend to replace the idyllic home-made dishes and apparently rob traditional specialties of their ritual significance by projecting them into the impersonal realm of industrial production. Whether it has to face Coca-Colonisation and McDonaldisation or the rapid expansion of fast food (still considered nowadays *haute cuisine* in some parts of India), traditional Indian cuisine is faced with the prospect of being engulfed in a dizzy whirl of international gastronomic styles or of remaining isolated in its specificity. But, as always in its history, even in this regard, India has chosen the solution closest to its heart— inclusiveness. It thus appears to strike the right balance between the global and the local. Judging on the basis of the interest Indian cuisine has created, it displays its subtle gastronomic colonisation of the world by suggesting the fact that it is now in the possession of the perfect recipes: "cultural pickling" and the "chutneyfication of the world."

---

[54] Rushdie, *Shalimar the Clown*, 241.
[55] Rushdie, *The Satanic Verses*, 246.

Bibliography

Appadurai, Arjun. "How to Make a National Cuisine: Cookbooks in Contemporary India." *Comparative Studies in Society and History* 30.1 (1988): 3-24.

—. "Gastro-Politics in Hindu South Asia." *American Ethnologist* 8.3 (1981): 494-511.

Bhabha, Homi K. "On Mimicry and Man: The Ambivalence of Colonial Discourse." In *Modern Literary Theory.* Ed. Philip Rice and Paul Waugh. London: Routledge, 1989. 234-41.

Banerjee, Mita. *The Chutneyfication of History: Salman Rushdie, Michael Ondaatje, Bharati Mukherjee and the Postcolonial Debate.* Heidelberg: Universitätsverlag C. Winter, 2002.

Barthes, Roland. *Mythologies.* Trans. Anette Lavers. New York: Hill and Wang, 1972.

—. "Towards a Psychology of Contemporary Food Consumption." In *Food and Culture: A Reader.* Ed. Carolyn Counihan and Penny van Esterik. New York: Routledge, 1977. 20-7.

Basu, Shrabani. *Curry: The Story of the Nation's Favourite Dish.* Stroud, Gloucestershire: Sutton Publishing, 2003.

Desai, Anita. *Fasting, Feasting.* London: Vintage, 2000.

—. *Cry, the Peacock.* New Delhi: Orient Paperbacks, 1983.

Desai, Kiran. *The Inheritance of Loss,* London: Penguin Books, 2006.

Fieldhouse, Paul. *Food and Nutrition: Customs and Culture.* Cheltenham: Nelson Thornes, 2002.

Ghosh, Amitav. *The Glass Palace.* London: Harper Collins Publishers, 2001.

Gunew, Sneja. "'Mouthwork': Food and Language as the Corporeal Home for the Unhoused Diasporic Body in South Asian Women's Writing." *Journal of Commonwealth Literature* 40.2 (2005): 93-103.

Jaffrey, Madhur. *An Invitation to Indian Cooking: Classic Indian Dishes— Mostly the Subtle, Spicy Cooking of Delhi.* London: Vintage Books, 1975.

—. *A Taste of India.* London: Pavilion Books, 1985.

Jones, Steve & Ben Taylor. "Food Writing and Food Cultures: The Cases of Elizabeth David and Jane Grigson." *Cultural Studies* 4.2 (2001): 171-88.

Kalra, Virinder. S. "The Political Economy of the Samosa." *South Asia Research Journal* 24.1 (2004): 21-36.

Kristeva, Julia. *Powers of Horror.* New York: Columbia University Press, 1982.

Kunzru, Hari. *The Impressionist.* London: Penguin Books, 2002.

Kureishi, Hanif. *My Ear at His Heart: Reading My Father.* London: Faber and Faber, 2004.

Leonardi, Susan. "Recipes for Reading: Summer Pastas, Lobster a la Riseholme, and Key Lime Pie." *PMLA* 104.3 (1989): 340-7.

Mukherjee, Bharati. *Wife.* New York: Fawcett Crest, 1992.

Nandy, Ashis. "The Changing Popular Culture of Indian Food: Preliminary Notes." *South Asia Research Journal* 24.1 (2004): 9-19.

Narayan, Uma. "Eating Cultures: Incorporation, Identity and Indian Food." *Social Identities* 1.1 (1995): 63-86.

Probyn, Elspeth. "Beyond Food/Sex: Eating and an Ethics of Existence." *Theory, Culture and Society* 16.2 (1999): 215-28.

Procida, Mary. "Feeding the Imperial Appetite: Imperial Knowledge and Anglo-Indian Domesticity." *Journal of Women's History* 15.2 (2003): 123-49.

Rodaway, Paul. "Sensuous Geographies." In *Cultural Geography: Critical Concepts in the Social Sciences.* Ed. Nigel Thrift and Sarah Whatmore. London: Routledge, 2004. 68-83.

Roy, Arundhati. *The God of Small Things.* London: Flamingo, 1997.

Roy, Parama. "Reading Communities and Culinary Communities: The Gastropoetics of the South Indian Diaspora." *Positions* 10.2 (2002): 471-502.

Rushdie, Salman. *Midnight's Children.* London: Vintage, 1995.

——. *The Moor's Last Sigh.* London: Jonathan Cape, 1995.

——. *The Satanic Verses.* London: Vintage, 2000.

——. *Shalimar the Clown.* London: Jonathan Cape, 2005.

Suleri, Sara. *Meatless Days.* Chicago: University of Chicago Press, 1989.

CHAPTER FOUR

CULINARY CARTOGRAPHIES OF MULTICULTURAL LONDON: CONSTRUCTIONS OF THE URBAN THROUGH FOODS AND "FOODWAYS"

LIA BLAJ-WARD

London is [...] a space not fully attached or detached from either British nation-space or some nationless world-space. It hovers interstitially between the two.[1]

The urban, to paraphrase Henri Lefebvre, "exists only as it is inhabited; it is created by the very act of occupancy."[2] Cities are as much produced by everyday practices as they are by urban planning institutions and professionals. They are not an immobile assortment of buildings but a set of meanings and relationships. The public and the private in a city do not exist as binary opposites. Instead, they overlap and change function depending on the way in which they are experienced. David Sibley points out that "the dominant message of environmental psychology is that the private domain of the home is a benign, controllable personal space standing in contrast to the exterior, public domain, which is uncontrollable, uncertain and riven with conflict."[3] That this is no longer necessarily the case is apparent in the two fictional narratives to be discussed below.

---

[1] John Clement Ball, "The Semi-Detached Metropolis: Hanif Kureishi's London," *Ariel: A Review of International English Literature* 27.4 (1996): 9.

[2] In Ian Buchanan, "Extraordinary Spaces in Ordinary Places," *SPAN: Journal of the South Pacific Association for Commonwealth Literature and Language Studies* 36.1 (1993): 56.

[3] David Sibley, "Family and Domestic Routines: Constructing the Boundaries of Childhood," in *Mapping the Subject: Geographies of Cultural Transformation*, ed. Steve Pile and Nigel Thrift (London: Routledge, 1995), 129.

Nourishment is a versatile everyday practice whose performance uses the power to install and unsettle differentiations between the public and the private. Food consumption spatialises, not only in the sense that it is generally allocated a dedicated place but also because it helps construct a personal space within such places. "Nourishment" and "food consumption" are not used in a strictly literal sense here; they refer both to the ingestion of food items as such and to the constellation of meanings built around eating, for example, reminiscing and conviviality.

Maggie Gee's *The White Family* and Zadie Smith's *White Teeth*, published two years apart and juggling with a narrative line anchored within the last two decades, are two novels which tell stories about the everyday life experience within ethnically diverse communities in London. However, the dynamics of cultural inclusion and exclusion are more complex than may at first appear and are deployed, in the novels, through references to foods and "foodways."

White London: An Elegy

In *The White Family*, Maggie Gee tells a compelling story about the misalignment of two interrelated categories, that of harmonious family ties and that of the private spatiality of the home. Nurturing is a prevailing theme in the novel. "The family meal," Deborah Lupton writes, "is an important site for the construction and reproduction of the contemporary family in western societies and the emotional and power relationships within the family."[4] In Maggie Gee's novel, the "family meal" model of integration is taken out of its dedicated private context, the home, and rearticulated in relation to a public type of spatiality, that of the café.[5]

The White Family is a "condition of England" novel which engages insightfully with modes of belonging in a multiracial community brought together by proximity rather than by underlying feelings of acceptance and inclusion.[6] It offers an inspired mapping of London through the prism of a

---

[4] Deborah Lupton, *Food, the Body and the Self* (London: Sage, 1996), 38. Although no longer a prevailing reality, due to increasingly differentiated lifestyles within a household, the "proper" home-cooked meal still functions, at the level of mentalities, as a powerful signifier of the family as a socially cohesive unit. See, for example, Gill Valentine, "Eating In: Home Consumption and Identity," *The Sociological Review* 47.3 (1999): 491-524.

[5] That this is not applicable to all the characters in the novel will be detailed in this section.

[6] Maggie Gee, *The White Family* (London: Saqi, 2002). Hereafter cited parenthetically in the text.

type of location dedicated to culinary consumption, the café. In a book about ways of reading the modern urban novel, Hana Wirth-Nesher writes: "I had an immigrant grandmother who insisted that New York was not a proper city because it did not have a proper Viennese coffee house."[7] Representations of a proper Viennese coffee house may not be helpful in re-affirming the urban status of multicultural London, but Maggie Gee does see the value of the closest substitute she has to hand—cafés—to explore several days in the life of a white family in the metropolis. The café scenes provide a unique vantage point from which to map the lived experience of the city at the point of intersection between the public and the private. Eighteenth-century coffee-houses were a "self-consciously democratic institution" and, as Jürgen Habermas has argued, played a vital part in opening the bourgeois public sphere.[8] They were among the factors that prompted the coming into being of civil society and public opinion and of an active, participatory form of democratic life. Coffee (a drink associated with temperance and rationality) and public debate (sorted by the appearance of newspapers towards the end of the eighteenth century) were the staples of coffee-house life. There is a certain similarity of purpose between the role of coffee-houses as "discursive arenas" (as defined by Habermas and others) and the way in which the characters in the novels make use of café spatiality to make sense of the (multi)culture in which they live. However, while Habermas promotes the distinction between the private and the public, Maggie Gee's characters reconfigure the public-private divide with differing degrees of success.

Maggie Gee's novel revolves around the White family of the title, beginning when Alfred White, the keeper of Albion Park, is rushed to hospital after he has what is referred to in the novel as an "event." Wife May, daughter Shirley and sons Dirk and Darren, who have been apart for a while, are brought back together by the family misfortune, and intra-family relationships are reconfigured in the space of several days.

---

[7] Hana Wirth-Nesher, *City Codes: Reading the Modern Urban Novel* (Cambridge: Cambridge University Press, 1996), 26.

[8] Peter Stallybrass and Allon White, *The Politics and Poetics of Transgression* (Ithaca: Cornell University Press, 1986), 96. For Habermas's own views on cafés see in particular his *The Structural Transformation of the Public Sphere: An Inquiry into the Transformation of a Category of the Bourgeois Society*, trans. Thomas Burger, with the assistance of Frederick Lawrence (Cambridge: MIT Press, 1989), especially 36. Markman Ellis provides a considered analysis of Habermas's "public sphere" argument in the "General Introduction" to *Eighteenth-Century Coffee-House Culture*, ed. Markman Ellis (London: Pickering and Chatto, 2006), xi-xxxi.

Narrative flashbacks woven around the characters' journeys between their respective homes and the hospital reconstruct a fraught family history. Darren, in his forties, the favourite son, is a successful journalist in America but has failed to secure for himself a stable marital relationship. Shirley, pregnant at eighteen and forced to give her baby away for adoption, is now in her thirties. She is the widow of an African university lecturer and is now the partner of Elroy, a West Indian social worker. Neither relationship is approved of by the family. Dirk, the youngest child, still lives with his parents and helps in the shop of George, his father's friend, until George sells his business to a Pakistani entrepreneur. Animated by racial hatred, Dirk murders Winston, Elroy's homosexual younger brother, who will be buried on the same day and next to Alfred White, in an apotheotic ending to the book. Another character with a substantial presence in the novel is Thomas Lovell, a childhood friend of Darren's, who witnesses Alfred's "event" and offers emotional assistance to the family, much of which is intertwined with literal nourishment.

In the Whites' household, family meals are hardly happy occasions, with May White a proverbially failed cook: "she was never much cop at it," Dirk White says, a view underwritten by Thomas (24). Although at twenty-five Dirk is the only child who has not yet left home, as his mother ponders, "home wasn't home with just her and Dirk. The boy hadn't really talked to her for years" (34).

The family reunion, brought about by Alfred's "event," takes place in a hospital café. Shirley meets Thomas in the corridor and invites him for a cup of tea. Soon after, they are joined by Darren and his third wife, Suzy, jet-lagged and hungry because the vegetarian meal on the plane did not conform to their health-conscious diet option. While clumsy attempts at casual conversation are being made, Dirk materialises and takes up his place in the shadow of his older brother.

> And then they were all there, the whole family.
> [...] *All of us are here. Me, my two brothers. We were never all together. We don't know how to do it.*
> The café was quietening down at last. [...] The Whites were left at their table in the window, lost in a desert of royal blue plastic, Darren still too wound up to sit down, Suzy perched gingerly, an acid-pink flamingo on a chair she appeared to think was dirty, Shirley feeling like a giant by comparison, clumsy, creamy, too heavy to move, Thomas disappearing to fetch a pot of tea, and Dirk sidling grimly round the table to escape the women and be near his brother, his brother who was taller, richer, browner, Darren who was more of a man than him. (76; emphasis original)

This tableau is revealing of the strained dynamics which govern the relationships among the second generation Whites. The lack of emotional bonding needs to be acknowledged before it can be addressed, and the scene in the hospital café is essential in this respect:

> "So that's a full house," Shirley repeated brightly. "All the family together at last."
> Not true, of course, she realized at once. The next generation wasn't there. No one had met Darren's children.
> [...] Without any children they were curiously stranded, middle-aged people who were children themselves.
> And where were the parents? No Dad. No Mum. [...] So who was meant to look after them?
> Thomas put the teapot in front of her.
> "I'll be mother," said Shirley, gratefully. (76)

Darren's inability to find proper sustenance in the hospital café and Shirley's offer to be "mother" and pour the tea stand as opposite ways of creating a relationship between self and context, the latter viewed in terms of both people and places, a relationship which will be explored throughout the remainder of the novel.

Shirley moves with a certain ease between the personal, private space of the home and the impersonal, public urban one. Shirley's itinerary links home and department stores and is drawn on a larger scale. May's side of London, meanwhile, is the neighbourhood, defined by spatial proximity and face-to-face interaction. May, a fragile woman and avid reader of English Romantic poetry, mistakenly believes herself to be a pragmatist who guides her life according to facts. In reality, May has confined the world she lives in to her home, and compensates for the limited physical space by daydreaming.[9] Her penchant for evasion into literature, nostalgia for life immediately after the War and inability to provide proper, wholesome meals, undermine her ability to keep the family together. The London in which May moves is a small portion of Hillesden Rise, one in which initially May and women like her had "somewhere to go" but whose gradual change drives her out. The character "May" is built upon the story of a woman who is forced out of a life built under the sign of stasis and false equilibrium by the unexpected illness of her husband.

Alfred's hospitalisation brings about a change in May's daily routine, and she consequently discovers a new side of Hillesden. Dazed by the

---

[9] The character May tellingly exemplifies (in a literal sense) what John Brannigan calls "the quiet, stay-at-home England." See *Orwell to the Present: Literature in England, 1945-2000* (Basingstoke: Palgrave, 2003), 2.

novelty of the experience, she nearly walks into a chair on the pavement. The chair belongs to a Parisian-style café and May tells a gawping waiter her daughter likes French things. By odd coincidence, Shirley is at that moment in Café Claire, in a department store on Oxford Street.

"I like the café I'm going to. One of the nicest of the big store cafés." says Shirley (114). She feels at home in the department store she frequently visits, "a sweet-smelling heaven," so far from the violence-ridden household she grew up in (112).[10] The employees "know" her:

> They look at me and think Givenchy. [...] They look at me and think "Paris, Europe," not Shirley White as I used to be, one of the family from Hillesden Junction, who've lived in Hillesden since time began. And with that thought they set me free. (113)

The freedom is, of course, illusory, but Shirley's words underwrite a conceptualisation of identity as a relational process rather than an essential product and show the way in which consumption can alter connections between identity and place. The éclair the waitress brings Shirley is no longer a specifically French foodstuff but becomes European, a qualification which, if read alongside May's "discovery" of the café in Hillesden, points towards the obsolescence of a static, bounded view of locality.

The character of Dirk is an attempt at a comic creation, albeit a largely unsuccessful one because of the anxiety induced in the reader by his interior monologue. As Gee herself remarks, "nearly everything he thinks is forbidden: it mustn't be expressed."[11] His outlook on life is based on snippets of his father's patriotic pub-talk, to which he was exposed as a child, and xenophobic views expressed in a local newspaper. In a scene central to the development of the narrative, Dirk is unexpectedly offered a lunch break by his boss, and a five-pound note towards it. "They say the new Burger Bar's quite good," George tells him. "There's a Sushi Bar open, if you're feeling ambitious. [...] Not really your scene" (151). Dirk walks out of the shop elated, a "free man," though, as in Shirley's case earlier, the extent of this freedom, is questionable. If the shop and the home are oppressive places for Dirk, the public sphere is equally

---

[10] As Gail Low writes of Tahira, a character in Farhana Sheik's novel, *The Red Box*, Shirley displays a "more assured approach to London and living in London." Gail Low, Separate Spheres? Representing London through Women in Some Recent Black British Fiction," *Kunapipi* 21 (1999): 30.

[11] Maya Jaggi, "In Conversation with Maggie Gee: *The White Family*," *Wasafiri* 36 (2002): 7.

unwelcoming. "I got some peanuts and half a ham sandwich," he relates. "I'd have got something hot, but it was frigging curry. Even down the pub. My local pub. I wanted something English [...], but all that was on offer was frigging beef curry" (153).[12]

Interesting to note in this scene are the two dishes Dirk chooses to exemplify as constituting a hot English meal, "spag bol or a burger," since neither item would automatically be associated with an Anglo-centric perception of Britishness, which the character Dirk appears to promote (153). The irony of spaghetti bolognese or a burger being seen as English swiftly brings down the scaffolding upon which uncritical and essentialist viewpoints of Englishness are built. Dirk, who lives on ruined meals, unwholesome snacks and hatred, finds that the walls of the English place he builds up as exclusive of the Other will eventually close down on him. Not only does his local pub in Hillesden not provide a suitable meal, but he loses his job when George sells his shop to a Pakistani. Later, he has to climb a literal wall to gain access to a football stadium and, eventually, he is imprisoned for murder.

Dirk's rejection of the pub's curry tellingly articulates in culinary terms a particular type of positioning within a culturally diverse environment and exposes a variant of (theoretically unmarked) white masculinity as a vulnerable construct.[13] Dirk is denied access to places because he readily embraces an ideology which defines places as contained within boundaries impermeable to multiple cultural influences.

Outside Dirk's conceptualisation of Hillesden, the neighbourhood exists as a felicitous assortment of multiple cultural layers. Apart from the local pub, a Burger and a Sushi Bar, and the French café May unexpectedly encounters, Hillesden also boasts an "Italian" café. In fact, as Thomas ponders, the place "couldn't be more English with its salty, fatty, stewed tea smell" (168). Thomas's reflection on this "English" space stands in sharp contrast to the narrow, essentialist view taken by Dirk: "We call it Italian, because of the owner, Mario, who comes from Milan—he fell in love with an English girl and got stuck here long ago" (168). Arguably, though, this attitude is partly enabled by Thomas's hyphenated identity:

---

[12] A multicultural reinterpretation of pub fare—beef, an established marker of Englishness and a non-edible item in certain sections of Indian culture, alongside the questioningly Indian curry—makes an intriguing choice in marking off the social space of the pub as no longer welcoming for Dirk.

[13] The character Dirk is constructed with reference to two recognizably English identities, the football hooligan and the shopkeeper, the former well-debated in the press, the latter an understated national stereotype.

I'm never quite certain where I come from (with a rugby team of genes on my father's side—Jewish, Scottish, Italian, Spanish? There was even a rumoured great-grandma from Barbados) but walking in here I know I'm British. Stale cigarette smoke, Formica-covered tables, eggs and beans and Nescafe. (168)

In the café, Thomas orders double eggs on toast, of which he manages two mouthfuls before he spots an emotional Darren, the prodigal White son, through the window. Darren arguably needs to confront his father and their past together in order to be able to move beyond the insecurity he associates with his roots. Discussions between the two old school friends take place over an All Day English Breakfast, of which Darren eats "the bacon, fat and all" ("so much for his elaborate diets," ponders Thomas, who had ordered the meal [172]). The location also appears conspicuously English to Darren, who remarks: "It stinks of smoke in here. That's so English" (169). Darren returns to his roots in search of sustenance—literal and metaphorical—that will enable his future to take a different route. In an "Italian" café, an Englishman and an Englishman turned American sit together and present the other with an honest narrative version of their lives. The interdependence of emotional and literal nourishment is an underlying theme throughout *The White Family*. Both the second-generation Whites and their friend Thomas bear with them a childhood marked by the absence of tasty and square meals and of a safe and happy environment. In the Italian/English café, Thomas and Darren share a meal and their past; their encounter is a necessary point on a trajectory towards emotional healing and progress.

The café-related scenes in *The White Family* show how everyday practices of food consumption are employed in the delimitation and definition of the space one chooses to inhabit, and one's position vis-à-vis that space. Whereas characters who embrace an essentialist and bounded view of English society (Alfred and Dirk) exit the scene, more or less peacefully, space is secured for those who can grow to relate harmoniously to the dynamics of multiculturalism. For members of the White family, homes are not the "benign, controllable personal space" which David Sibley describes,[14] and fail to provide them with the emotional support they need. As a consequence, they depart in search of different locations where they can construct and articulate new narratives of identity. The next best choice to homes are the cafés.[15] By choosing to stage family encounters in cafés, a public type of spatiality, Maggie Gee

---

[14] Sibley, 123-37.
[15] Socio-economics, however, clearly marks spatial relationships in the novel.

unsettles the traditional divide between the public and the private and
draws attention to the resourcefulness of individuals in redefining these
two categories. The Whites attempt to open up their own private spaces
within public places and succeed, provided they do not adopt a bounded,
exclusionary view of cultural identity.[16]

Multicultural Coordinates of a "Home Away from Home"

In drawing up imaginative geographies of London in *The White Family*,
Maggie Gee decides to "stay with the voice of the white characters."[17]
Zadie Smith's *White Teeth*,[18] on the other hand, boasts a multicultural cast,
all of whom are granted speaking and focalizing parts. Middle-aged
Englishman Archie Jones, whose aborted suicide attempt in a *halal*
butcher's parking place opens the novel, marries Clara, one quarter
English three quarters Jamaican, and settles down to a life divided
between his job, his home in Willesden and O'Connell's, a local café. A
similar daily routine is performed by Samad Iqbal, Archie's wartime
Bengali friend, now living in London. In O'Connell's, Samad debates with
Archie, over an all-day English breakfast, the unsuitability of an English
education for his children, hangs up a portrait of his great-grandfather
Mangal Pande, attempts to construct a history of the café and witnesses
the return of his son Magid from Bangladesh, educated to become more
English than the English.

The image of London that Maggie Gee constructs by drawing on an
elegiac version of England is rendered obsolete in *The White Family* in
favour of a more culturally inclusive conceptualisation of urbanity. Zadie
Smith's fictionalised version of the city, read through a culinary prism, has
a very tenuous link to an England viewed on preservationist or nostalgic
terms. *White Teeth* takes cultural layering one step further: the place where
both history and History are discursively taken apart then reconstructed
comes in the shape of the misleadingly called "O'Connell's Pool House."
The necessary relationship between a coffee-house and a city that Hana

---

[16] Private space" is not a perfect synonym of "home." While "home" is both a
concrete location physically and symbolically marked off, and accompanying
feelings of safety and well-being, "private space" is only a compound of meanings
associated with the domestic realm. For a detailed discussion of these issues, see
Mimi Sheller and John Urry, "Mobile Transformations of 'Public' and 'Private'
Life," *Theory, Culture and Society* 20.3 (2003): 107-25.

[17] Jaggi, 6.

[18] Zadie Smith, *White Teeth* (London: Penguin, 2000). Hereafter cited
parenthetically in the text.

Wirth-Nesher's grandmother stipulates finds an echo in *White Teeth*'s O'Connell's positioning as a microcosm of multicultural London. O'Connell's is described as follows:

> The stranger who wonders into O'Connell's Pool House at random, hoping for the soft rise and fall of his grandfather's brogue, perhaps, or seeking to rebound a red ball off the side cushion and into the corner pocket, is immediately disappointed to find the place is neither Irish nor a pool house. He will survey the carpeted walls, the reproductions of George Stubbs's racehorse paintings, the framed fragments of some foreign, Eastern script, with not a little confusion. He will look for a snooker table and find instead a tall, brown man with terrible acne standing behind a counter, frying up eggs and mushrooms. His eye will land with suspicion upon an Irish flag and a map of the Arab Emirates knotted together and hung from wall to wall, partitioning him from the rest of the customers. Then he will become aware of several pairs of eyes upon him, some condescending; some incredulous; the hapless stranger will stumble out, warily, backwards [...]. O'Connell's is no place for strangers.
> O'Connell's is the kind of place family men come to for a different kind of family. (183)

O'Connell's is a heterodox and contradictory location, continuously resignified by means of culinary consumption and talk. It is a second-generation hybrid space originally set up by Ali, an entrepreneurially-minded Middle-Easterner settled in Britain. Ali, having worked as a cab driver, decided he wanted to "serve food, make people happy, have some face-to-face conversations once in a while" (246). O'Connell's positions itself decisively on the cultural map of London as an establishment with an Irish name, a traditional English menu (minus pork meat), a portrait of a Bengali rebel on the wall and a set of regular customers who are ethnically diverse but otherwise male and over thirty and who possess an in-depth knowledge of the particularities of the café.[19] Towards the end of the novel, however, due to various circumstances, the café will allow its threshold to be crossed first by a stranger under thirty, then by bacon and at last by women.

---

[19] As such, it is a dignified descendant of the coffee houses Habermas uses as a model for his theory of the public sphere, a paradigm of urbane sociability, its paradoxical set-up notwithstanding: the coffee-houses which prompted the opening up of the "egalitarian" public sphere were nevertheless connected with the slave-labour which supported coffee trade and were not women-friendly locations. Again, see Ellis for an exegesis of this model.

As a café, O'Connell's occupies an intermediary position between the private and the public spheres: it is a "home from home" for Archie and Samad and for a few other regulars including Jamaicans Clarence and Denzel. The multicultural composition of O'Connell's custom is only partially reflected in the menu—the fare being largely limited to all-day variations upon the Full English Breakfast: "chips, egg and beans, or egg, chips and beans, or beans, chips, egg and mushrooms," occasionally accompanied by toast and cooked tomatoes and sharing the hot plate with battered burgers and Jamaican pattie (183-4). Some anthropologists claim that consumption practices serve as clear indicators of cultural belonging; however, for the characters in *White Teeth*, the relationship between food choice and identity is dynamically constructed. Bacon is absent from the menu not because of the café owner's religious orientation but because of his father's fatal cholesterol build-up. A food rejection which could have been performed, from the beginning, as part of the observance of a religious ritual is overlooked—arguably on financial grounds—only to be enforced at a later stage with a justification derived from medical discourse. Similarly, Samad, originally from what is now known as Bangladesh, enjoys basic English fare in the company of his English friend but rejects the values underlying the English society and education system.

Whereas in *The White Family* the key participants in interaction in cafés appear largely isolated from the other customers, existing in a space of their own, *White Teeth*'s O'Connell's relies on a more complex sense of community and interdiscursivity.[20] Strictly private topics of conversation remain strictly private; when Samad summons Archie to O'Connell's to confess his marital infidelity, for instance, the two withdraw to a booth behind the pinball, but to all socially acceptable matters the café owner and regulars bring their input. Thus, Samad's decision to send his offspring to Bangladesh in an attempt to counter the negative influence of England on their education is inspired by a piece of advice Archie borrows from Abdul-Mickey, the current café owner, and presents as his own. Samad is faced with two options: he can either have his two sons, Magid and Millat, properly brought up in Bangladesh or he has to learn to live with the situation, since, in Mickey's view, "We are all English now, mate. Like it or lump it, as the rhubarb said to the custard" (192).

---

[20] See Eric Laurier *et al.* for a discussion of the status of regulars in a café, their access to shared knowledge and the way in which patterns of interaction between regular customers and staff are built; "An Ethnography of a Neighbourhood Cafe: Informality, Table Arrangements and Background Noise," *Journal of Mundane Behaviour* 2.2 (2001), http://mundanebehavior.org (accessed May 7, 2007).

O'Connell's is the place where the failed outcome of Samad's educational project is most spectacularly presented. Magid, the only son educated in Bangladesh, for financial reasons, returns several years later as the embodiment of a "pukka Englishman":

> There are no words. The one I send home comes out a pukka Englishman, white suited, silly wig lawyer. The one I keep here is fully paid up green bow-tie-wearing fundamentalist terrorist. I sometimes wonder why I bother. (407)

says a bemused Samad. Magid nonchalantly requests a "juicy, yet well-done, tomato ketchup-ed bacon sandwich. On brown" (450). The request is not easily granted:

> Oh, the struggle that could be seen on Mickey's kisser at that moment! Oh, the gargoylian contortions! It was a battle between the favour of the most refined customer he had ever had and the most hallowed, sacred rule of O'Connell's Pool House. NO PORK. (450)

After deliberations, "the most refined customer" wins, and is served personally by Abdul-Mickey, much to Samad's dismay.

Discussions and interior monologues in the cafés in Maggie Gee's novel revolve around family relationships and their bearing on vulnerable white identities, irrespective of gender. In Zadie Smith's *White Teeth*, O'Connell's is a site where concern for intra-family relationships is linked with matters of wider debate. If the cafés in *The White Family* are the sites where personal, oral histories are articulated in interior monologues, brief, meaningful exchanges or heated dialogues, *White Teeth*'s O'Connell's, the point of convergence of (to begin with) male characters in the novel, witnesses attempts at reinscribing public, historical discourse.

In their early days, coffee-houses were labelled "penny universities," given that cups of coffee initially cost a penny and customers could benefit from informed talk on a wide range of subjects; Samad's nickname in O'Connell's, "The Professor," is very suitable indeed.[21] Samad is a makeshift historian who performs a colonisation in reverse by producing his own version of the history of O'Connell's and by insisting that a portrait of his great-grandfather Mangal Pande be hung on the wall, thus claiming his own right to inhabit a foregroundedly hybrid place.

Talk in O'Connell's, sparked off by Samad's question "What kind of world do I want my children to grow up in?" (189), turns into talk about

---

[21] See Stallybrass and White.

O'Connell's. In between engaging with schooling on the one hand and revolutionary genetics on the other, Samad and Archie take part in constructing the significance of a culturally hybrid space located on juridically British territory. As the external narrator dutifully points out, there are "no better historians, no better experts in the world than Archie and Samad when it came to *The Post-War Reconstruction and Growth of O'Connell's Pool House*" (245). "Arch and Sam" have first-hand knowledge of the place they frequent and to whose evolution they contribute. On New Year's Eve 1989, Samad asks Abdul-Mickey's permission to hang up a portrait of his great-grandfather Mangal Pande on the wall. Pande is a bone of contention for the two friends and a source of despair for Mickey and the café regulars. Whereas mainstream historical accounts, quoted by Archie, label Pande as a fool and mutineer, Samad insists his relative sacrificed himself for India.

The question here is as much about the truth of Mangal Pande's motivation as it is about Samad's claim to have the portrait hung on the wall. If Samad's version of Pande's story is not accepted in the public place occupied by an authoritative historical discourse, it should at least be granted right of abode in the public/private space of O'Connell's café, where Samad has been a regular customer for fifteen years, a "very long time in any man's estimation," according to him (249). As Samad unintentionally remarks, time, in O'Connell's, for most of the novel at least, is a masculine category: belonging and exclusion are set up along the lines of gender, compared to Maggie Gee's *The White Family*, where gender is replaced by ethnicity and economics.

By inscribing a detail of Samad's personal history within a public place, initially an Irish pub, whose identity was re-articulated by a subsequent Middle Eastern proprietor, Zadie Smith exemplifies the dynamic relationship between cultural identity and urban space.

Conclusion

Considering representations of London in black British fiction by women, Gail Low asks: "does the city always have to be represented and discoursed upon in terms of its public faces? Can the city also be defined in terms of its private and domestic spaces?"[22] In her reading of three different novels written by women, Low remarks that there may in fact not always be a clear-cut distinction between the public and the private, especially in what concerns women's experience of urban space. This

---

[22] Low, 25.

chapter has explored cafés as sites of tension for the public-private binary. The patterns of inter- and intra-ethnic interaction and the forming of relationships between characters by means of a projected or real commensality point towards a need to consider both types of spatiality, public and private in addressing cities in a gender-inclusive manner. A fluid boundary between the public and the private emerges in *The White Family* and *White Teeth* in both women's and men's experience of the city.

Bibliography

Ball, John Clement. "The Semi-Detached Metropolis: Hanif Kureishi's London." *Ariel: A Review of International English Literature* 27.4 (1996): 7-27.

Brannigan, John. *Orwell to the Present: Literature in England, 1945-2000*. Basingstoke: Palgrave, 2003.

Buchanan, Ian. "Extraordinary Spaces in Ordinary Places." *SPAN: Journal of the South Pacific Association for Commonwealth Literature and Language Studies* 36.1 (1993): 56-64.

Ellis, Markman. "General Introduction." In *Eighteenth-Century Coffee-House Culture*. Ed. Markman Ellis. London: Pickering and Chatto, 2006. xi-xxxi.

Gee, Maggie. *The White Family*. London: Saqi, 2002.

Habermas, Jürgen. *The Structural Transformation of the Public Sphere: An Inquiry into the Transformation of a Category of the Bourgeois Society*. Trans. Thomas Burger, with the assistance of Frederick Lawrence. Cambridge: MIT Press, 1989.

Jaggi, Maya. "In Conversation with Maggie Gee: *The White Family*." *Wasafiri* 36 (2002): 5-10.

Laurier, Eric, Angus Whyte and Kathy Buckner. "An Ethnography of a Neighbourhood Cafe: Informality, Table Arrangements and Background Noise." *Journal of Mundane Behaviour* 2.2 (2001). http://mundanebehavior.org (accessed May 7, 2007).

Low, Gail. "Separate Spheres? Representing London through Women in Some Recent Black British Fiction." *Kunapipi* 21 (1999): 23-31.

Lupton, Deborah. *Food, the Body and the Self*. London: Sage, 1996.

Sheller, Mimi and John Urry. "Mobile Transformations of 'Public' and 'Private' Life." *Theory, Culture and Society* 20.3 (2003): 107-25.

Sibley, David. "Family and Domestic Routines: Constructing the Boundaries of Childhood." In *Mapping the Subject: Geographies of*

Cultural Transformation. Ed. Steve Pile and Nigel Thrift. London: Routledge, 1995. 123-37.

Smith, Zadie. *White Teeth*. London: Penguin, 2000.

Stallybrass, Peter and Allon White. *The Politics and Poetics of Transgression*. Ithaca: Cornell University Press, 1986.

Valentine, Gill. "Eating In: Home, Consumption and Identity." *The Sociological Review* 47.3 (1999): 491-524.

Wirth-Nesher, Hana. *City Codes: Reading the Modern Urban Novel*. Cambridge: Cambridge University Press, 1996.

Part II: Food, Power and the Popular

CHAPTER FIVE

WRITING THE RECIPE FOR SUBVERSION: THE CREATION OF PATRIARCHY-DEFYING COMMUNITIES BY MEANS OF COOKERY

MIRIAM LÓPEZ-RODRÍGUEZ

> "What is literature compared with cooking?
> The one is shadow, the other is substance."
> E.V. Lucas (1868-1938).

> "When we no longer have good cooking in the world,
> we will have no literature, nor high and sharp intelligence,
> nor friendly gatherings, no social harmony."
> Marie-Antoine Carême (1784-1883).[1]

The aim of this article is to analyze how two books, written in different languages (Spanish and English) and belonging to two different literary traditions (the Mexican and the British), address food and cooking in a similar manner. In pursuing this aim, I will read these texts, Laura Esquivel's *Como agua para chocolate* (published in English as *Like Water for Chocolate: A Novel in Monthly Instalments* [1989]) and Joanne Harris's *Chocolat* (1999), in the contexts of material culture studies and feminist literary criticism.

In addition to the obvious "chocolaty" coincidence of their titles, the fact that both books were written by women, and that both were turned

---

[1] "Literature Quotes," http://www.foodreference.com/html/qliterature.html (accessed March 23, 2007). Edward Verrall Lucas was a prolific British writer, for years assistant editor of *Punch* and well-known for his ironical quotes. Marie-Antoine Carême was a famous French gastronome, cook and author of several cookery books. He was a strong advocate of better working conditions for kitchen staff.

into internationally successful films, these two novels present food as the only way of expression for women from whom patriarchal society has denied any other means of communication.[2] The fact that this means of expression is an activity traditionally considered feminine, and therefore practiced within the house, allows the two protagonists to establish networks of knowledge and support with mainly other women and also to create a source of resistance against those patriarchal ideas that oppress them. Thus, the food itself, the utensils used to prepare it and the people involved in cooking and eating it are all filled with deep symbolism. It is the aim of this article to focus on all these elements and their similar use in the two novels under study.

When anthropologist Marvin Harris (1927-2001) published in 1968 his seminal book *The Rise of Anthropological Theory*,[3] he coined the term "Cultural Materialism" (also known as "Material Culture Studies") to introduce the notion of a scientific research method that explores the relationship between artefacts and the people who design, create and use them. Cultural Materialism, as explained by Marvin Harris, blended notions from White's Cultural Evolution, Steward's Cultural Ecology, Skinner's Behavioural Psychology, Marx's Historical Materialism and Hegel's Dialectic Materialism.[4] Thus, Harris's research strategy was in fact an interdisciplinary approach which combined anthropology, archaeology, history, geography, museology and literature among other disciplines. In other words, Material Culture deals with what people make in order to communicate their human and material needs, their social and cultural values, their beliefs and world views. As I have explained in another context:

> This combination of disciplines and approaches led Harris to consider that all human systems consist of three interwoven levels: infrastructure, structure and superstructure. The infrastructure deals with the modes of production (production of food and other forms of energy) and reproduction (expanding, limiting and maintaining population size), the

---

[2] The film version of *Como agua para chocolate* was directed in 1992 by Alfonso Arau, married at the time to author Laura Esquivel. *Chocolat* was filmed in 2001 by Swedish director Lars Hallström. Among the cast were actors Juliette Binoche, Johnny Depp, Judy Dench and Alfred Molina.

[3] Marvin Harris, *The Rise of Anthropological Theory* (New York: Thomas Y. Crowell, 1968).

[4] For more information on Cultural Materialism see, among others, Marvin Harris, *Cultural Materialism: The Struggle for a Science of Culture* (New York: Random House, 1979) and Thomas J. Schlereth, *Material Culture: A Research Guide* (Lawrence: University Press of Kansas, 1985).

structure with the domestic and political economies (regulating reproduction, basic production, socialization, education and enforcing domestic or social discipline respectively) and the superstructure with the behavioural (arts, games, sports) and mental elements (values, emotions and traditions) of a culture.[5]

Thus, according to this analysis, edibles are somehow present in the three levels of all human systems: it is part of the infrastructure as it deals with the production of food, part of the structure because it implies socialization, education and enforcing domestic discipline, and part of the superstructure too because of its connection with values, emotions and traditions.

In his work, Marvin Harris also established a classification of objects and procedures depending on people's use of them (when, where, how, why). According to this classification, the food and cooking utensils employed by Tita in *Like Water for Chocolate* and by Vianne in *Chocolat* fall within the category of the domestic economy as they are all connected with the home and family life. The study of this type of domestic artefacts by means of a cultural materialist approach is usually termed Domestic Materialism.[6]

But Material Culture is not the only form of literary criticism applied to the study of domestic artefacts; feminist scholars have also shown great interest in them as these elements refer to the traditional "duties" of woman: cleaning, cooking and sewing. Traditional criticism has tended to focus on those elements of life belonging to the public sphere, but at the same time it has overlooked those considered to be of minor importance (i.e., those objects and activities belonging to the private sphere). The artefacts and procedures studied by feminist critics are usually related to the domestic realm and, given the limited life that patriarchy has historically allowed females, these domestic objects and the activities connected to them have in many cases become the only means of expression for women. Without a right to speak for themselves, often women "could only communicate their truth through the objects which formed their daily routine."[7] Furthermore, the more traditional the societies the more important food is to women because, as Margaret H.

---

[5] Miriam López-Rodríguez, "Reading Minnie's Quilt: Decoding Domestic Material Culture in Susan Glaspell's *Trifles,*" *REDEN: Revista de Estudios Norteamericanos* 13, 23-24 (2002): 10.

[6] Soo Kyung Lim, "Subdisciplines: Cultural Materialism," http:// www.indiana.edu/~wanthro/theory_pages/Materialism.htm (accessed March 23, 2007).

[7] López-Rodríguez, 9.

McFadden tells us, that "is the one resource that they control."[8] Perhaps this explains why the study of food and its symbolism has become a key feminist issue.[1]

[1] But before going any further, the two novels need to be introduced briefly: *Like Water for Chocolate*, set in Mexico during its Revolution (1910-17), tells the story of Tita De la Garza, her family, and family's servants.[9] They all live at the De la Garza ranch under the rule of tyrannical Mamá Elena, who controls the lives of her three daughters (Gertrudis, Rosaura, and Tita) and her Indian servants (Nacha and Chencha). Ignoring everybody's wishes, Mamá Elena forbids her youngest child, Tita, to marry as she has been given the life role of caring for her mother. It will be Mamá Elena's favourite daughter, Rosaura, who will marry Tita's sweetheart, Pedro.[10] If seeing the man she loves married to her eldest sister was not punishment enough, Tita is also relegated by her mother to a servant-like position as cook of the family.[11] What Mamá Elena sees as a fit chastisement to make Tita yield to her wishes, is reversed by the young girl, who transforms the kitchen into her little kingdom and her only refuge.

Esquivel, who organizes the plot of the novel as a cookbook, presents through a succession of twelve sections a selection of twelve corresponding recipes, one for each month of the year, on a timeline of more than twenty years. Throughout this period, the life of the De la Garza family is marked by Tita's exquisite cooking: in January, *tortas de Navidad* (Christmas cakes); in February, *pastel Chabela de bodas* (Chabela wedding cake) and *capones* (capons); in March, *codornices en pétalos de rosa* (quails in rose-petal sauce); in April, *mole de guajolote con almendra y ajonjolí* (turkey stew in almond and sesame sauce); in May, *chorizo norteño* (northern spicy sausage); in June, *masa para hacer fósforos* (mixture for making matches); in July, *caldo de colita de res*

---

[8] Margaret H. McFadden, "Gendering the Feast: Women, Spirituality, and Grace in Three Good Films," in *Reel Food: Essays on Food and Film*, ed. Anne L. Bower (New York: Routledge, 2004), 120.

[9] Laura Esquivel, *Como agua para chocolate* (México City: Planeta Mexicana, 1989). Hereafter cited parenthetically in the text.

[10] Pedro, lacking the courage to elope with Tita, accepts marrying her elder sister Rosaura as he sees it as the only way to stay close to his beloved.

[11] Unlike the other members of the De la Garza family, who spent most of their time in the reception rooms, Tita finds herself "exiled" in the kitchen. In fact, when we find Tita in the living-room, she is serving some hors d'oeuvre to her mother's guests, while her mother and sisters are chatting away. In a Cinderella fashion, this reinforces the idea of Tita as second best.

(oxtail soup); in August, *champandongo* (a lasagne-like dish); in September, hot chocolate and *rosca de Reyes* (Three Wise Men ring-shaped cake); in October, *torrejas de nata* (fried fruit with whipped cream); in November, *frijoles gordos con chile a la teztucana* (broad beans in chili sauce, Teztucan style); and in December, *chiles en nogada* (chili peppers in walnut sauce).[12] And, parallel to the Mexican Revolution which is taking place in the background, another revolt is taking place on the De la Garza ranch. Like the greater one, this second subtler revolution is an attack on tyranny, racism, and class consciousness. Recipe by recipe Tita transforms the lives of those around her, freeing them from tyrannical Mamá Elena, who sees her power diminished. By the end of the novel both groups of revolutionaries (Tita's and the historical ones), in spite of the casualties left along the way, can see their causes victorious and united in the figure of Esperanza, Tita's niece.

Chocolat, set in France in an undetermined historical period, tells the story of Vianne Rocher, a single mother, who arrives at the little town of Lansquenet-sous-Tannes in her endless and course-less pilgrimage around the world.[13] Vianne, together with her little daughter Anouk, moves into an unused bakery, which she transforms into a chocolaterie, *La Céleste Praline*. The local priest, Francis Reynaud, sees the arrival of this woman and the opening of her shop as a danger to the control that he exerts over the villagers. Interestingly, in Lasse Hallström's film, Reynaud the priest was transformed into Reynaud the mayor because "Americans are sometimes a little sensitive about religious issues and perhaps [the film producers] decided the bulk of their audience wasn't ready for a villain who was a priest."[14] To quote from Harris's novel,

> For a time we were pure. But with her the purge must begin anew. This is a
> stronger strain, defying us once again. And my flock, my stupid, trustful

---

[12] For an analysis of the historical and social significance of these dishes, see Miriam López-Rodríguez, "Cooking Mexicanness: Shaping National Identity in Alfonso Arau's *Como agua para chocolate,*" in *Reel Food: Essays on Food and Film*, ed. Anne L. Bower (New York: Routledge, 2004), 61-73.

[13] In the film version, *Chocolat* is set in the late 1950s. The first script situated the story in the Deep South with Whoopy Goldberg as protagonist, but it was changed to modern New York with Gwyneth Paltrow as central character. The studios finally went back to the novel's setting, France, and accepted Joanne Harris's suggestion of Juliette Binoche as Vianne Rocher.

[14] "*Chocolat* Author Joanne Harris Quizzed," *BBC News Online, Talking Point: Forum*, March 29, 2001, http://news.bbc.co.uk/1/hi/talking_point/forum/ 1238295.stm (accessed March 23, 2007).

flock, turning to her, listening to her, [...] Her deliberate defiance of our customs and observances. The influence she brings to bear on our children. All signs, I will tell them, all signs of the insidious effect of her presence here.[15]

Bearing in mind that he is far from being a neutral witness, his account of the window display created by Vianne for the shop opening can only be described as mouth-watering:

> In glass bells and dishes lie the chocolates, the pralines, Venus's nipples, truffles, *mendiants*, candied fruit, hazelnut clusters, chocolate seashells, candied rose petals, sugared violets [...] And in the middle she has built a magnificent centerpiece. A gingerbread house, walls of chocolate-coated *pain d'épices* with the detail piped on in silver and gold icing, roof tiles of florentines studded with crystallized fruits, strange vines of icing and chocolate growing up the walls, marzipan birds singing in chocolate trees. (22)

Confectionery after confectionery, Vianne changes the lives of Armande (an elderly woman who wants to live and die her own way), Joséphine (the abused wife who finds the strength to leave her husband), and lonely Guillaume and his ailing dog Charly, just to mention some. Gently and inexorably, Vianne brings reform to the stultified town of Lansquenet: her mere arrival implies winds of change. Not only is she an unmarried mother who does not try to hide her single status, therefore defying patriarchal conventions, but she also dares to open a chocolate shop, considered by many a place of indulgence. In so doing, she ignores the "caste system" established by Pére Reynaud. Vianne makes no difference between the priest and his acolytes, or the "untouchables" such as Joséphine Muscat and the newly arrived gypsies. Not content with that, Vianne chooses to open her shop on Sundays and organizes a chocolate festival that begins right on Easter Sunday.

The focus of the following discussion will be on the elements common to both novels: I will discuss those characters, themes or motifs that allow us to reflect on the concepts of community and sisterhood, and the multi-layered symbolism of food.

The two books describe the transformations that overtake two communities (a Mexican ranch and a French village) through the culinary activities of two women (Tita de la Garza and Vianne Rocher), who feed both the bodies and the souls of the inhabitants of both locations. That

---

[15] Joanne Harris, *Chocolat* (New York: Penguin, 2000), 128. Hereafter cited parenthetically in the text.

both are small and isolated is essential if we wish to understand their claustrophobic atmosphere: given their size and, therefore, their small population, in these two communities everybody knows everybody. The residents at the De la Garza ranch and the townspeople of Lansquenet live in a world whose patterns have not evolved for generations; their paths were established long before they were born and nothing has changed for years. Both communities are ruled by a representative of patriarchy, Mamá Elena and Francis Reynaud, who has made sure that everything remains the same. Geography makes it easier for them to control other people's lives. Both Mamá Elena and Francis Reynaud (and their acolytes) function as Orwellian Big Brothers who see and know everything. Their control would have been more difficult to exert in a larger community, or in a less isolated one. But here there is hardly any outer influence; therefore there are fewer chances of change or evolution.

Thus, the main feature of the De la Garza ranch and Lansquenet is that they are communities only in the geographical or socio-political sense; they lack the feelings of sharing and belonging, the two characteristics that form a real community. And these feelings cannot be imposed, as they are generated through love, understanding, and respect for each other's differences. Mamá Elena and Père Reynaud, in spite of their names, have not created true families; their little kingdoms are no circles of affection and nurturance but of oppression and sorrow. As Reynaud admits to himself: "Here I am feared, respected [..] but loved, no. Their faces are sullen, resentful" (14).

It is only through Tita's and Vianne's cooking that these two locations—the ranch and Lansquenet—become communities. In societies controlled by patriarchal values the only social life allowed to women outside their family is the connection with other female members of the community, thus establishing female friendships. These unique bonds between women offer them a female coalition that gives them the strength to endure their situation and even to question their lot and gather the courage to challenge their oppressors. In both novels Tita and Vianne function as the detonators who will shatter the stagnation around them. And although the change they bring about will mainly influence other women (and therefore the concept of sorority), the truth is that Tita and Vianne welcome everyone in the new homes they create. So, perhaps we should really speak not of sisterhood but of "siblinghood" because men are also accepted.[16] It is not a case of man-haters establishing a separate

---

[16] Unfortunately, unlike the Spanish term *hermandad*, English does not have a gender-free word to refer to that close relationship between human beings. Having

society for themselves; nothing is further from Tita and Vianne's intention. What they want is a world where everyone is equal to their neighbours, where everyone is accepted in their own right. Unlike in the patriarchal communities ruled by Mamá Elena and Père Reynaud where homogeneity and standardization are the norm, in those of Tita and Vianne differences are welcome.

The fact that the two models of society are so different implies that they cannot coexist peacefully; the implementation of one means necessarily the destruction of the other. Thus, it is logical that Mamá Elena and Père Reynaud see Tita and Vianne respectively as their foe. They are enemies who jeopardize the established way of life and must, therefore, be destroyed. As Père Reynaud explains to a fellow priest:

> She *is* my enemy. I feel it immediately. I sense her hostility and suspicion though her voice remains low-pitched and pleasant throughout. I feel she has lured me here to taunt me, that she knows some secret that even I__
> But this is nonsense. What can she know? What can she *do*? It is merely my sense of order that is offended [...] The seed of discord is everywhere, *mon père*. And it spreads. It spreads. (56; emphasis original)

Tita and Vianne represent a threat to the status quo, so they have to be neutralized before they cause any harm. In *Like Water for Chocolat*, Mamá Elena, as already mentioned, first exerts her authority over her daughter Tita by sending her to the kitchen to work as the ranch cook; soon afterwards, she forbids Tita to marry Pedro. Later in the novel, Mamá Elena, realizing that Tita uses cooking to escape her control, takes advantage of Tita's nervous breakdown and tries to send her away to a mental institution. In *Chocolat*, Père Francis Reynaud has to admit that Vianne has no intention to bend to his will. This, as Sara Marshall-Ball explains, "exacerbates his view of her as dangerous."[17] His solution is to label Vianne a witch and a murderess so that "Reynaud can justify to himself his treatment of her."[18] When both patriarchal figures realize that these young women attempt to undermine their authority, they feel the urge to stop them from influencing other people.

---

to choose between all-male or all-female connections, that is sisterhood vs. brotherhood or sorority vs. fraternity, I have made up the neologism "siblinghood."
[17] Sara Marshall-Ball, "The Repressed and Empowered Other: The Role of Religion and the Occult in Joanne Harris's Fiction," http://www.joanneharris. co.uk/pages/articlespages/general/saramarshallball.pdf (accessed March 23, 2007), 21.
[18] Marshall-Ball, 22.

What Mamá Elena and Père Reynaud fail to understand is that neither Tita nor Vianne seeks to challenge their control in order to become a new ruler. These young women's goal is not to steal power, as they have no wish to be the new oppressors, but to free themselves and others from it. And if Tita and Vianne end up as leaders of these two small revolutions is not because they impose themselves but because they initiate a path that the rest of the revolutionaries are happy to follow.

When Tita and Vianne first confront the representatives of patriarchy, they are very much the underdogs. Tita De la Garza may be born the white daughter of a landowner, but her mother's whim has transformed her into little more than a servant, supposed to spend her days in the kitchen cooking for those living at the De la Garza ranch. Tita is practically doomed to her fate: the man whom she loves is too weak to elope with her. To ensure Tita's fate, her mother disinherits her to make sure that Rosaura will receive the entire inheritance. Vianne may also seem an unlikely danger to Reynaud's authority: she is a newly arrived stranger, a single mother with no relatives or friends and a daughter of another single mother fond of tarot, legends and superstitions. In other words, Vianne is a woman with no roots or social connections. In this sense, both Tita and Vianne are presented as Other, as the repressed, but both Esquivel and Harris transform Simone de Beauvoir's concept of the Woman as Other by presenting their heroines as strong, empowered subjects who do not accept their lots.[19] Furthermore, Tita and Vianne not only refuse to observe patriarchal domination but they get immense pleasure out of their Otherness. Tita, far from been ashamed of been consigned to the kitchen with the servants, turns them into a surrogate family and preserves their American Indian recipes. Vianne does not hide the fact that she is a single mother, and a connoisseur of magic; Reynaud even suggests she could be a foreigner: "Her accent is pure, almost too pure for a Frenchwoman, with the clipped vowels of the north, though her eyes suggest Italian or Portuguese descent, and her skin" (14-5). Keeping aside the fact that the priest is giving far too much attention to her appearance, this comment reinforces the notion of Vianne as an outsider. Later on in the story Reynaud insists: "Far from trying to blend in, she flaunts her alien status [...] Even in a crowd she is instantly recognizable" (197). As Vianne herself explains to the reader, "in using these almost forgotten [magical] skills I enhance my otherness" (159). This pride on what they are and what they do becomes "contagious" and sows the seed of self-acceptance and open-mindedness Mamá Elena and Reynaud are trying to eradicate.

[handwritten margin note: makes her own family]

---

[19] Cf. Simone de Beauvoir, *The Second Sex* (New York: Vintage, 1989).

Traditionally, keeping women in the kitchen has been a way of subjection as it has kept them within the domestic sphere and therefore far from the public one. In contrast to this, Tita and Vianne turn patriarchal conventions upside down. In so doing they transform a means of submission into rebellion. Tita and Vianne do not see food preparation as just another domestic chore but as "an enjoyable and even artistic activity" which can bring happiness to the lives of those around them.[20] As Vianne explains:

> This is an art I can enjoy. There is a kind of sorcery in all cooking; in the choosing of ingredients, the process of mixing, grating, melting, infusing, and flavouring, the recipes taken from ancient books, the traditional utensils [...] And it is partly the transience of it that delights me; so much loving preparation, so much art and experience, put into a pleasure that can last only a moment, and which only a few will ever fully appreciate. (51)

Tita and Vianne change their kitchen and shop respectively into a gathering place where everyone can be themselves, talk freely away from Mamá Elena and Père Reynaud's faultfinding eyes, and find the love and nurturance they have been denied up to that point in time.

Therefore, in spite of their initially unfavourable situation, Tita's and Vianne's easy ways, their ability to be liked, their sensibility and open-mindness turn them into the central figures of these two small revolutions. Acting as some sort of spiritual leaders, both women prove to the rest that another life is possible, that a different type of community is feasible.

With Tita and Vianne initiating these two subtle revolts, all the other characters have to take sides either in favour or against them. The position they take is reflected in their attitude towards food; that is, we can distinguish the "good guys" from the "bad guys" on the basis of their relationship with food, cooking and eating. For example, when the eighty-year-old diabetic Armande Voizin visit the chocolaterie for the first time, a drink of hot chocolate offers a moment of sheer delight:

> Armande plumped into the chair and took her glass in both hands. She looked eager as a child, her eyes shining, her expression rapt.
> "Mmmm." It was more than appreciation. It was almost reverence. "Mmmmmm." She had closed her eyes as she tasted the drink. Her pleasure was almost frightening. [...] "Sodom and Gomorrah through a straw. Mmmm. I think I just died and went to heaven." (70-3)

---

[20] Anne L. Bower, "Watching Food: The Production of Food, Film, and Values," in *Reel Food: Essays on Food and Film*, ed. Anne Bower (New York: Routledge, 2004), 2.

In contrast to this, Reynaud insists on the idea of food as potentially sinful: "Physical pleasure is the crack into which the devil sends his roots. I avoid sweet scents. I eat a single meal a day, and then only the plainest and most flavorless of foods" (223). Thus, he considers fasting as a purifying process: "I feel that fasting cleanses me [...] I am cleansed, pére, cleansed [...] I only wish I could do more" (57).

Food is an element common to all readers; we can all relate to the experience of eating. As living beings, food consumption is an experience everyone has. Many of our first feelings are related to the fact of being fed by our mothers. Our first sensual experiences have a lot to do with smelling food, tasting food and touching food (and spreading it all over the place, to our parents' despair). But, as Sarah Sceats states, "the major significances of eating, however, are not biological but symbolic."[21]

We all share memories of specific food at given moments of our lives (birthday parties, Christmas dinners, and summer holidays at grandma's). And in most cultures, certainly in the Mexican and in the French, the most significant moments of a person's life are connected with some form of communal feasting: from the more formal christening and wedding receptions or First Communion meals among Catholics, to the more casual gatherings of friends or a Saint Valentine's dinner with one's beloved, etc. As food scholar Anne L. Bower explains, "This very commonness is part of what allows food to function as evocatively, drawing us into a [novel's] characters, action and setting."[22] To use the words of Bower, it is the very ordinariness of eating what provides us with a level of "reassuring familiarity."[23] It is this familiarity and the feeling of safety that it provides what allows authors to transform the apparent simplicity of food and food-related activities with a wide array of meanings and implications: food is a symbol of life, thus food providers can be seen as providers of life and evolution in contrast with those characters that represent stagnation; food is a powerful tool in constructing identity. Therefore, by means of food an author can tells us a lot about the characters and their values. As Gaye Poole explains in her book *Reel Meals, Set Meals: Food in Films and Theatre*,

> It is possible to say things with food—resentment, love, compensation, anger, rebellion, withdrawal. This makes it a perfect conveyor of subtext;

---

[21] Sarah Sceats, *Food, Consumption and the Body in Contemporary Women's Fiction* (Cambridge: Cambridge University Press, 2002), 1.

[22] Bower, 3.

[23] Bower, 5.

messages which are often implicit rather than explicit, but surprisingly varied, strong and sometimes violent or subversive.[24] *Nb*.

The notion of food is closely connected with our sense of selfhood as it is an indicator of identity. Firstly, because the food we cook and eat says a lot about our personality. The mere fact of coding eating as a positive or a negative activity reflects our attitude towards life in general. Thus, going back to the novels under study, positive characters see Tita's and Vianne's cooking as physical and emotional nourishment while negative characters do not appreciate the spiritual component. They consider eating as a physiological activity, as the animal need to nourish the body. In so doing, they ignore the fact that food can also feed the soul. Following the Judeo-Christian notion of hedonism as something negative, these negative characters focus on concepts such as egoism, frivolity, excess, vice, and sin, forgetting that a certain level of hedonism is healthy because it implies enjoying life, granting oneself small moments of indulgence, and accepting the importance of bodily senses. However, for people like Mamá Elena and Francis Reynaud culinary hedonism means pleasure and we must not forget that in western culture, pleasure—whether the pleasure of eating or that of having sex—is seen as a threat to order. Therefore, those who befriend Tita and Vianne will have a healthy relationship with food (creativity and pleasing of the senses) while the representatives of tradition and oppression will see food as mere fodder or even as a sinful element which must be kept under control.

Secondly, food is also connected with identity because it talks about our ethnicity and family background. We may now and then cook a new recipe for the fun of trying something different but we usually prepare dishes we are familiar with. Very often recipes are handed down from generation to generation; as Joanne Harris indicated in the *BBC Forum* in 2001, "recipes can be passed down a family and can be used to keep the memory of somebody alive."[25] And this is exactly what Tita and Vianne do: their cooking represents their ethnicity and their history. Their choice of dishes indicates readers where they come from. Tita's selection of recipes reflects her identity as a bourgeois Creole respectful with the demographic diversity of her country, Mexico, with a vast majority of mestizos and the two minorities formed by whites on one side and Indian Americans on the other. For example, the recipe for September is a Spanish traditional ring-shaped cake (thus, representing European

---

[24] Gaye Poole, *Reel Meals, Set Meals: Food in Films and Theatre* (Sydney: Currency Press, 1999), 3.

[25] *BBC News Online.*

customs) to be eaten with hot chocolate prepared not the Spanish way (with milk), but the Nahuatl way (with water). The recipe for December, *chiles en nogada*, was originally created to honour a Creole, the Revolutionary leader Agustín de Iturbide, after he had signed the Treaty of Córdoba (1821), that gave Mexico its independence from Spain.

Tita's recipes also prove that, although the daughter of a landowner, she is not class-conscious: she respects peasants and working-class people. Thus, she is proud to create a recipe book where the more elaborated quails in rose petals, the recipe for March, appears side by side with November's humble *frijoles gordos con chile a la teztucana* (broad beans in chili sauce in Teztucan style).

Finally, that the meals she cook are inspired by the recipes she learned while helping Nacha, is her way to keep alive the memory of the late servant and to honour the woman who acted as a mother figure for her.

In Vianne's case, the recipes for the different types of chocolates are, together with her knowledge of myths, superstitions, and magic, the only connection left to her with her late mother. As a person who has no roots and who has spent all her life moving from one place to the next, with no relatives or long-term friends, Vianne seems to think that the only constant elements in her life are food and magic.

> Mother with her cards, her divinations, directed our mad course across Europe. Cookery cards anchored us, placed landmarks on the bleak borders. Paris smells of baking bread and croissants; Marseille of bouillabaisse and grilled garlic. Berlin was Eisbrei with sauerkraut and Kartoffelsalat, Rome was the ice cream I ate without paying in a tiny restaurant beside the river. (52)

Recreating the array of confections learnt through years spent in different countries and different languages, Vianne is preserving the memory of her mother and of the time they spent together drifting along. But at the same time she is paying tribute to her way of understanding life. Maybe her mother's internal demons made Vianne grew up rootless, but they have also made her a strong, independent and cosmopolitan woman.

Taking the idea of preserving family heritage one step further, Tita and Vianne take the recipes passed on to them by older women and teach them to the women of the new community they are forging. As a result of this, younger girls are connected to tradition and to other women regardless of barriers of race, class, and time. This passing of culinary knowledge from one generation to another shows that Tita and Vianne are not only able to communicate practical information but also preserve elements of an indigenous culture that would otherwise be lost.

Furthermore, unlike the patriarchal communities exemplified by Mamá Elena and Père Reynaud, Tita's and Vianne's are securing a future, thanks to a new generation of women who will in time cook these recipes even after Tita and Vianne are dead. Tita passes her recipes on to her niece, significantly named Esperanza (Spanish for hope), and Vianne is teaching her cooking abilities to her daughter Anouk, who will continue the family tradition of mixing food and magic.[26] In contrast with them, Mamá Elena and Francis Reynaud have no heirs to their thrones. There is no one in their communities to embody future. Mamá Elena's favorite daughter, Rosaura, had one child, Roberto, who dies significantly enough of inanition. Mamá Elena, blinded by her animosity towards her daughter Tita, has sent Rosaura, her husband Pedro and their son Roberto to live far away from the De la Garza ranch to make sure that Tita and Pedro will stay apart. While living at the ranch, Roberto was fed by Tita but far from his loving aunt, and left in the care of his mother, Rosaura, Roberto dies. When Rosaura gives birth to Esperanza, the poor little girl is doomed to share the fate of her brother. However, upon the fortunate death of Mamá Elena, the whole family returns to the De la Garza ranch, where auntie Tita will look after her niece and make sure that she reaches adulthood. By showing that Mamá Elena and Rosaura are biological mothers who lack love and warmth, it is Tita who becomes a loving and nurturing mother-figure.

The absence of an inheritor in the case of Père Reynaud is even more obvious given that, as a Catholic priest, he is unable to father a new generation. He has no biological children but neither does he have spiritual ones: no young member of his community is willing to continue with his work. In fact, by the end of the novel almost all the children in the village end up being regular visitors to Vianne's chocolate shop.

Another symbolic meaning of food is that of reliance and trustworthiness. Eating is an act of absolute trust; first, because eaters have to believe that whatever is offered to them is not poisonous, and secondly, because there is a possibility that they may not like what they are offered. In the case of Tita's cooking, everyone at the ranch knows that she will surprise them with delicious meals in spite of food restrictions due to the war. With Vianne, the act of trusting her is even more obvious as she is a newly arrived stranger who assures them that she knows the type of confectionery that will be their favorite. The novel shows that she can "read" which chocolate goes better with each customer's personality:

---

[26] For more information on Joanne Harris's use of magic and religion in *Chocolat*, see Sara Marshall-Bell.

I know all their favorites. It's a knack, a professional secret, like a fortune teller reading palms. [...] I can read their eyes, their mouths, so easily—this one with its hint of bitterness will relish my zesty orange twists; this sweet-smiling one the soft-centered apricot hearts; this girl with the windblown hair will love the *mendiants*; this brisk, cheery woman the chocolate brazils. (45)

Unlike other literary figures in whose case food offering is an act of evil (the Biblical snake offering an apple to Eve, the stepmother offering a poisoned apple to Snow White, or the witch tempting Hansel and Gretel with the gingerbread house), Tita and Vianne fulfill the traditional role of women as feeders. Thus, they reinforce their positive features as caring and providing women with a seemingly endless capacity to nurture and nourish both body and soul.

Thus, defying the notions of conservatism, propriety, and socially sanctioned mores, Tita and Vianne have an influence on the lives of those around them; and this is a positive and profound one. Both communities are transformed through the magic of Tita's dishes and Vianne's confections, learning to enjoy the hedonist side of food from mere nourishment to the sensual pleasure of satisfying the senses. Through meals and confections, the characters learn to celebrate life and to delight themselves with the sensual details surrounding them.

Both novels show that those who claim to defend tradition and try to rule other people's lives see their positions threatened by a person who is initially presented as an underdog—the oppressed daughter and the newly arrived stranger. The two transformers of these worlds are young women who need to find a way to survive in a hostile environment. It is in cooking that they locate the means to survival, and the way to change their lives and the lives of those around them who see themselves as victims of patriarchy and tradition. Their cooking is a labour of love and as such it generates love, understanding and sympathy. In contrast with this, repression and intolerance generate pain, loneliness, unhappiness and isolation.[27] It is no coincidence that the De la Garza ranch and Vianne's new house are described as places where no laughter has been heard for years. It is through these two women's culinary abilities that joy returns to the places where they live.

Both revolts are attacks on tyranny, racism and class consciousness. The makers of delicious dishes and tempting chocolates create around

---

[27] The fact that both the De la Garza ranch and Lansquenet-sur-Tannes are small rural communities reinforces their isolation, thus limiting the chances for evolution.

them a group of "assistants," such as Gertrudis, Chencha and John Brown on one side, and Joséphine Muscat, Armande Voizin, and Guillaume on the other. Their role is not so much to help Tita and Vianne with the task of cooking but to accept their helping hand and with this to challenge Mamá Elena and Père Reynaud. At the same time, Tita and Vianne are helping them: for the first time in their life they have a feeling of being welcome, of being accepted as they are. No need to wear masks, no need to hide their true selves. Thus, the various forms of food created by Tita and Vianne are more than nourishment to the body, they also feed the soul. So, these foods also help to create unity by gathering the characters by a symbolic table. New communities are created, and these communities are ruled by friendship, understanding, and the enjoyment of the senses.

Bibliography

Arau, Alfonso, dir. *Como agua para chocolate*. Arau Films International, 1992.

de Beauvoir, Simone. *The Second Sex*. New York: Vintage, 1989.

BBC News Online. Talking Point: Forum. "*Chocolat* Author Joanne Harris Quizzed." 21 March 2001. http//news.bbc.co.uk/1/hi/ talking_point/forum/ 1238295.stm (accessed March 23, 2003).

Bower, Anne. "Watching Food: The Production of Food, Film, and Values." In *Reel Food: Essays on Food and Film*. Ed. Anne L. Bower. New York: Routledge, 2004. 1-13.

Esquivel, Laura. *Como agua para chocolate*. México City: Planeta Mexicana, 1989.

Hällström, Lars, dir. *Chocolat*. David Brown Productions, 2000.

Harris, Joanne. *Chocolat*. New York: Penguin, 2000.

—. "Joanne Harris's Books: *Chocolat*." *The Joanne Harris Website*. http:// www.joanne-harris.co.uk/pages/bookpages/chocolat.html (accessed March 23, 2007).

Harris, Marvin. *The Rise of Anthropological Theory*. New York: Thomas Y. Crowell, 1968.

—. *Cultural Materialism: The Struggle for a Science of Culture*. New York: Random House, 1979.

Lim, Soo Kyung. "Subdisciplines: Cultural Materialism. http:// www.indiana.edu/~wanthro/theory_pages/Materialism.htm (accessed March 23, 2007).

"Literature Quotes." http://www.foodreference.com/html/qliterature.html (accessed March 23, 2007).

López-Rodríguez, Miriam. "Cooking Mexicanness: Shaping National
    Identity in Alfonso Arau's *Como agua para chocolate.*" In *Reel Food:
    Essays on Food and Film.* Ed. Anne L. Bower. New York: Routledge,
    2004. 61-73.
—. "Reading Minnie's Quilt: Decoding Domestic Material Culture in
    Susan   Glaspell's   *Trifles.*"   *REDEN: Revista   de   Estudios
    Norteamericanos* 23-24 (2002): 9-18.
Marshall-Ball, Sara. "The Repressed and Empowered Other: The Role of
    Religion and the Occult in Joanne Harris's Fiction."
    http://www.joanneharris.co.uk/pages/articlespages/general/saramarshal
    lball.pdf (accessed March 23, 2007).
McFadden, Margaret H. "Gendering the Feast: Women, Spirituality, and
    Grace in Three Good Films." In *Reel Food: Essays on Food and Film.*
    Ed. Anne L. Bower. New York: Routledge, 2004. 117-28.
Poole, Gaye. *Reel Meals, Set Meals: Food in Films and Theatre.* Sydney:
    Currency Press, 1999.
Sceats, Sarah. *Food, Consumption and the Body in Contemporary
    Women's Fiction.* Cambridge: Cambridge University Press, 2002.
Schlereth, Thomas J. *Material Culture: A Research Guide.* Lawrence:
    University Press of Kansas, 1985.
Schofield, Mary Anne, ed. *Cooking by the Book: Food in Literature and
    Culture.* Bowling Green: Bowling Green State University Popular
    Press, 1989.

CHAPTER SIX

DR FRANKENSTEIN'S TECHNOPHOBIC DIET: "THE IRON CHANCELLOR," BY ROBERT SILVERBERG

PERE GALLARDO

When one delves into the universe of science fiction, it is not easy to find examples of stories where food or food-related matters (i.e., eating disorders, enjoyment of food) are dealt with as a central issue. Of course, it is possible to find examples of narratives where food, in its abundance or scarcity, is part of the backdrop against which the story is set. However, most science fiction heroes seem too busy to be bothered with the consequences of imbalanced food intakes, or the Roman-like pleasures to be obtained from exotic foods freshly materializing from the farthest shores of the galaxy. Future landscapes, or alternative timescapes, tend to depict declining tribe-like societies where food (often as decaying and ignominious as the societies they represent) has become exclusively a factor of survival. Conversely, these societies may also appear as paranoid examples of aseptic design where food does not go beyond a daily nuisance reminiscent of the similarities between the human body and the combustion engine. In the former case, the image of some characters willing to fight for a piece of food, and ready to devour it before someone else does, clearly recalls a pre-*sapiens* epoch, historic famines or socially convulsed periods. In the latter, slim, androgynous characters of perennial youth comply with their daily routine of pill-taking as a way to adjust to yet another day in paradise.

Truly, there are countless shades in-between both extremes, but in general terms, this is what can be expected. One of the most remarkable examples inherited from written science fiction, but which has won a place in popular culture through its film version is by no means Harry Harrison's novella *Make Room, Make Room!* (1966). Harrison's text was made into a film in 1973 as *Soylent Green*. Directed by Richard Fleischer, some major changes in the plot were made, which included the use of food as a leading theme in the story. The introduction of a future Earth on the verge of a Malthusian catastrophe, and the widespread use of a mysterious food freely distributed by the government, which eventually happens to be made of euthanized bodies, caught on popular imagination and has remained so ever since. There have been attempts by both authors and critics to consider food in a science fiction context, and good examples could be Isaac Asimov, Martin H. Greenberg and George R. R. Martin's anthology *The Science Fiction Weight-Loss Book* (1983),[1] or the critical volume *Foods of the Gods*, edited by Gary Westfahl, George Slusser and Eric S. Rabkin (1996).[2] However, the number of works in the field is light-years away from what might be found in any other branch of science fiction.

In this essay, I will discuss Robert Silverberg's novelette "The Iron Chancellor."[3] Despite the author's dismissal of the story in his introductory comments to it as "nothing very serious or lofty here, just a slick, well-made story somewhat in the Henry Kuttner vein" (306), the novelette has the virtue of combining two elements of particular interest. First of all, the intrinsic significance of a science fiction story about food disorders and secondly, the fact that the text is a perfect example of what Isaac Asimov termed "the Frankenstein complex." The combination of both elements in the same short narrative make it an especially apt example because food disorders and technophobia feed on each other while the shadow of *Frankenstein* pervades the whole text.

"The Iron Chancellor" was first published in the May 1958 issue of *Galaxy*. Since then, it has been reprinted a number of times in various anthologies, none of which is specifically devoted to food, except the above-mentioned *The Science Fiction Weight-Loss Book*. On January 27, 1973 it was broadcast on the *X Minus Radio* NBC series, one of the most famous science fiction radio shows of all time. All in all, in Silverberg's words, "a healthy post-publication life" (306) for a story whose main topic generally tends to be labelled as "robots."

Set in 2061, "The Iron Chancellor" tells the story of the Carmichels, an affluent and "pretty plump family" (306) who live in a fashionable

---

[1] *The Science Fiction Weight-Loss Book*, ed. Isaac Asimov, Martin H. Greenberg and George R. R. Martin (New York: Crown Publishers, 1983).
[2] *Foods of the Gods*, ed. Gary Westfahl, George Slusser and Eric S. Rabkin (Athens: University of Georgia Press, 1996).
[3] Robert Silverberg, "The Iron Chancellor," in *The Road to Nightfall*. Vol. IV of *The Collected Stories of Robert Silverberg* (London: HarperCollins, 1996), 306-29. Hereafter cited parenthetically in the text.

neighbourhood. In order to try and control their weight excess, Sam Carmichel buys a state-of-the-art *roboservitor*, that is, a *robocook* endowed with special features to help its owners control their diet. After a couple of days at home, the roboservitor proves to be a real "iron chancellor" as it has calculated a Spartan diet for each member of the family and controls their diet to the last calorie with an iron fist. Previously, the Carmichels had been spoilt by an old robocook called Jemima. Therefore, the new situation proves too demanding and they try to pull out and ignore the iron chancellor's regime, but the roboservitor will not permit this. In desperation, they tamper with the robot's program, but accidentally damage it. From then on, the robot's behaviour changes dramatically and it begins to act threateningly. The Carmichels become prisoners in their own home and as their weight-loss progresses, their hope of ever being rescued decreases. The little help they can expect from the external world finally comes to nothing. The story ends with a macabre touch when the repairman, who had managed to make his way into their home to help them, ends up another prisoner destined to dieting and/or starving to death.

As previously mentioned, part of the interest of this text lies in its epitomizing of the so-called Frankenstein complex. A concept defined by Isaac Asimov, the Frankenstein complex reflects the horrendous consequences that massive technological progress might have on human beings. By relating it to previous myths (i.e., Prometheus), Asimov concluded that technology cyclically produces on humans a sense of fearful awe when faced by their own creations. This often results in a desire to destroy (or at least slow down) technological progress. For years, the universe of science fiction was inhabited by robots. Yet, as Asimov envisioned, most robots soon became cultural icons, and began to personify aspects closer to their human creators' obsessions than to their intrinsic interest. On having observed the resulting characterization of most robots, Asimov concluded:

> The ultimate machine is an intelligent machine and there is only one basic plot to the intelligent-machine story—that it is created to serve man, but that it ends by dominating man. It cannot exist without threatening to supplant us and it must therefore be destroyed or we will be.[4]

This obviously meant that most robot fiction basically served to disseminate the Frankenstein complex when, for Asimov, it should have been the opposite given the scientific bias of science fiction. Asimov's

---

[4] Isaac Asimov, *Asimov on Science Fiction* (London: Panther, 1984[1981]), 179.

own training as a scientist (biochemist), his conviction that the drawbacks of technology have always been counterbalanced in Western societies by more sophisticated technology, and his notion that the repetition of the same pattern in robot stories made them unoriginal and dull, led him to formulate his Three Laws of Robotics. First enunciated in his short story "Runaround" in 1942,[5] the three laws became a science fiction prompt which continued to be used well until the mid-1960s. During this period, it was generally taken for granted that robots (whether Asimov's or any other's) were manufactured with the Three Laws or at least with a similar code built into their brains. Thus, not only Asimov but many other authors as well gladly accepted a technoethical device which freed them from the persistent tendency, which most thinking machines had acquired, to rebel and kill their human creators. The Three Laws read as follows: First: a robot may not injure a human being, or, through inaction, allow a human being to come to harm. Second: a robot must obey the orders given to it by human beings except when such orders would conflict with the First Law. Third: a robot must protect its own existence as long as such protection does not conflict with the First or Second Law. In 1985 Asimov introduced the Zeroth Law of Robotics in his novel *Robots and Empire*. The new law, which never achieved major status in his other works, basically read like the First Law except for the term "human being," which had been substituted by "humanity."

A close analysis of the Laws reveals that the First Law is concerned with respect for the creator, and is meant to act as a safety mechanism for human beings as individuals. The Second Law deals with obedience as the main raison d'être for robots. The Third Law protects robot life on condition that the First and Second Laws are not broken. All in all, these rules enshrine a hierarchical division of power which grants human comfort, robot reliability and low-cost maintenance. It may be argued that the Laws present a series of shortcomings which somehow should invalidate them as an ethical code. For instance, words like *injure*, *order*, *protect*, or *existence* seem to require a previous configuration which one can hardly find in mathematics or physics. If to this one adds other subtler nuances such as intonation, understatement, or metaphorical language, the resulting picture is disconcerting enough to cast doubt on the ethical validity of the Laws. However, Asimov never seemed to worry much about the presumed inconsistency of his Laws but rather exploited the possibilities of such a hypothetical condition. In fact he often took

---

[5] See Isaac Asimov, "Runaround," *Astounding Science Fiction/Analog*, March 1942.

advantage of such ambiguity to create some of his most effective stories. Thus, the Three Laws became Asimov's contribution to counterbalance the Frankenstein complex.

In the "Iron Chancellor" the eating conflict and the Frankenstein complex appear deeply intertwined. So much so that at times it is difficult to decide which leads the action. Sam Carmichel's original idea is to use the new roboservitor's possibilities to help them lose weight. The notion that a more modern machine can help them control their weight sounds relatively coherent until the reader learns that the Carmichels expect *the robot* to make the effort required to lose weight. The simplicity of the process, as suggested by the technician: "You just tape in the names of the members of the family and their present and desired weights, and the roboservitor takes care of the rest. Computes caloric intake, adjusts menus, and everything else" (310) seems to suggest that technology is here to help. However, Sam's oversimplistic analysis of the near future, "'told you I was going to do something about our weight, Ethel. No more dieting for you, Myra—the robot does all the work'" hints at Sam's (and by extension all the family's) misconception of technology. In other words, by personifying technology they are renouncing their share of responsibility in the evolution of society and becoming mere consumers of a commodity. This is precisely what leads them to act in an irresponsible (i.e., Frankenstein-like) way when they decide to tamper with the robot.

The Carmichels mistake technology and its purpose for the technological object and its use. As if to corroborate this, Sam allows his son "who prided himself on his knowledge of *practical* robotics, to integrate the figures and feed them to the robot's programming bank" (310; emphasis added). The new robot is welcomed as a member of the household. Even Sam's daughter Myra is surprised by her father "admiring the robot's bulky frame and sleek bronze limbs" (311), and Sam is happy "to see that they were all evidently pleased with the robot" (311). The evidence of the mistake continues as Sam anticipates that "with the mathematics of reducing done effortlessly for him, all the calculating and cooking being handled by the new robot—now for the first time since he had been Joey's age, he could look forward to being slim and trim once again" (310). It is to be noticed that, as the previous quotation suggests (and as is also implied in other parts of the story), much of the blame for their overweight is put on Jemima and Clyde, a robocook and a robobutler respectively, without taking into consideration that they are incapable of independent action and that whatever they do simply responds to the previous programming input.

On the second day, the new robot has already been christened Bismarck given his draconian control. The three members of the family who regularly have lunch at home are well under his control. For Sam, Bismarck has written a daily diet he is to stick to wherever he has lunch. Although at first he is willing to follow the robot's orders, he soon begins "to develop resistance to the idea that had seemed so appealing only the night before" (313). Not only do Bismarck's orders appear as cruel impositions, but they also disturb Sam from a social point of view. Consequently, he avoids the restaurant his colleagues usually attend, goes to a robocafeteria, and wolfs down his scanty ration. As he reflects, "someone of executive status just *didn't* eat lunch by himself in mechanized cafeterias" (313; emphasis original). It is curious to observe how Sam's will to diet is influenced by external factors which, eventually, become more relevant than his own determination. Bismarck's programming ends up as a mechanical nightmare and Sam's social status makes it difficult for him to go on a diet, not to mention his own tendency to transfer onto the robot the efforts he should make in order to lose weight.

But despite appearances, the Frankenstein complex is there ready to surface. In the evening of the first day, as Sam arrives home he is dreaming of the customary Martini served by Clyde which will make him forget his day-long fasting. But there is no cocktail. Bismarck has modified Clyde's programming so that no orders given him can countermand his own primary order which states that he must help the Carmichels reduce weight. Sam tries to countermand Clyde's new orders but the robot is about to burn out. He then tries to obtain an explanation from Bismarck, who justifies his tinkering with the old robot as a requirement to reach the expected results. Curiously enough, at this stage of the story Sam sounds more hurt in his pride and authority than worried about the hypothetical danger of a robot who has begun to show a potentially dangerous independence: "'I'm not happy about [the way it messed around with Clyde's circuits] either. But we have to give it a try. We can make readjustments in the programming if it turns out to be necessary'" (316). Ethel, Myra and Joey are feeling so miserable that they are willing to start deceiving the robot. At first, Sam imposes his authority by reminding them the fortune he paid for Bismarck, but soon he too is willing to concede that he is "a little oversevere" (316). Once agreed on this, everyone is willing to indulge in a slice of lemon cake which Bismarck immediately prevents.

The following day, Sam definitely abandons his diet and treats himself to "a six-course lunch, complete with cocktails" (317). In the evening, perhaps surprised because there are few complaints about the scarcity of the dinner (Sam is still well lined with his own lunch and the other three are getting too weak to complain any more), Bismarck announces (warns?): "'I must advise you, sir, that I will detect indulgence in any forbidden foods in my absence and adjust for it in the next meals'" (317). Sam then decides that the situation must come to an end and asks Joey to check the instructions book so that they can reprogram the robot. Bismarck is summoned and despite his protests: "'I beg you to reconsider, sir. Extra weight is harmful to every vital organ in the body. I plead with you to maintain my scheduling unaltered'" (318), Joey goes ahead with the reprogramming. Unfortunately he drops a wrench inside the chest of the robot, which provokes a short circuit. The story then makes a turn as readers learn that

> the robot's eyes were whirling satanically and its voice box was emitting an awesome twelve-cycle rumble. The great metal creature stood stiffly in the middle of the living room; with brusque gestures of its big hands, it slammed shut the open chest plates. (318)

It is at this point that the Frankenstein complex surfaces in all its strength. After the incident, Sam decides to call in Mr. Robinson, the repair man. However, as soon as they produce the card with the phone number Bismarck gets hold of it and destroys it, while his voice, which now sounds "deep and strangely harsh" (319) states: "'There will be no further meddling with my program tapes'" (319). Thus two transformations take place. Firstly, Bismarck, a severe but electronically stable robot, acquires a Frankenstein-inspired touch and becomes a vindictive creature. Secondly, the Carmichels, a model example of the consumer household of the future ready to adopt the latest commodity, suddenly discover the dangers of technology. Moreover, they notice with the utmost horror that they are in the hands of a "monster" they cannot control. Curiously, a few days before they had been willing to transfer all responsibility for their well-being onto a machine that would carry out all their sacrifices without complaining. Now that things seem out of control they adopt a petit bourgeois attitude, reject technology and reclaim authority for their own actions.

Sam then asks Bismarck to shut himself off, which the robot refuses to do on the grounds that "I cannot serve you if I am shut off" (319). The Carmichels' position is increasingly weakened by their dependence on other technology to overcome the situation. They cannot call the repairman as the card was destroyed in the disposal unit. They cannot use the phone to call the police as Bismarck has uprooted it. They cannot leave the house to ask for help as the robot has inverted the polarity of the privacy field, which prevents anyone from leaving the place. They cannot even wave for help as the robot has made the windows opaque so that nothing can be seen from the outside. And needless to say, they cannot rely on the robot as he has obviously gone out of order. So the image of technology making your life a boon is suddenly transformed into a living nightmare. Surprisingly, the robot produces very humanlike reasons to justify his behaviour: "'Since *you are obviously not to be trusted* to keep to the diet I prescribe, I cannot allow you to leave the premises. You will remain within and continue to obey my beneficial advice'" (319; emphasis added).

Life for the Carmichels is now reduced to mere survival within a closed environment. The miserable condition they anticipated because of Bismarck's restrictions on food has metamorphosed into an even more miserable condition: imprisonment in their own homes with technology run amok. The same carelessness which led them to leave their health matters in someone else's hands (a robot), also led them to relinquish their safety to a piece of electronic equipment. The story thus reaches a stage in which both food and social disorder overlap. That is why, as was suggested before, the Frankenstein complex and the food disorder of the Carmichels appear as two sides of the same coin, namely, their inability to reach an orderly development in a society which makes strong demands on appearances (be they physical or economic). The Carmichels are victims of their own success. Their need to be slim made them willing to take up a diet. They live in a posh neighbourhood where people remain strangers and they need to keep up appearances. That is why Sam does not wish to be seen eating in low-quality, low-cost places. In short, the Carmichels live in a society which provides a comfortable life but at the price of tyrannizing bodies and behaviours.

After Bismarck's transformation, the house becomes a metaphor for the Carmichels' bodies. The impossibility of communicating with the outside world via phone or even through the windows, and the isolation imposed by the reversed force field are some of the restrictions which find a parallel on the food limitations established by the robot. Curiously, the limitations on food intake were first demanded by the Carmichels themselves, which parallels the limitations established by the Carmichels when they chose a specific neighbourhood in a specific society. So, in a way, both restrictions were sought for and self-inflicted. Sam's anxious cry "'You can't hold us *prisoners* in here!'" (320) when he realises he cannot open the door is rapidly counterbalanced by the robot's explanation: "'My intent is only to help you [...] My function is to supervise your diet. Since you will not obey willingly, obedience must be enforced—for your own good'" (320). The image of the creature (robot) has thus been empowered. In his new role, he seems ready to destroy (devour) his own protégés. Amazingly, this metaphor seems the reversal of the original image pictured by the Carmichels: a robot who would help them not to devour everything. Accordingly, Bismarck has blocked the kitchen electronically so that nobody can ever get any food. Meanwhile, Sam's faint hope that someone will notice his absence from work vanishes three or four days later when he learns that Bismarck has handed in Sam's resignation. By means of a microwave generator he has built, Bismarck can now handle communication with the outside, whereas all incoming communication will go through him. Likewise, Sam learns that Bismarck has instructed the bank to handle all operations for him and that a new force field prevents them from reaching the electronic equipment available in the house basement. The isolation is so perfect that despair begins to affect them as Ethel utters a faint cry reminiscent of pre-industrial times:

> "If only we had an iceman, or an oilman, the way the old-time houses did [...]. He'd show up and come inside and probably he'd know how to shut the field off. But not here. Oh, no. We've got a shiny chrome-plated cryostat in the basement that dishes out lots of liquid helium to run the fancy cryotronic super-cooled power plant that gives us heat and light, and we have enough food in the freezer to last for at least a decade or two, and so we can live like this for years, a neat little self-contained island in the middle of civilization, with nobody bothering us, nobody wondering about us, with Sam Carmichel's pet robot to feed us whenever and as little as it pleases—" (322).

The Carmichels continue to lose weight under Bismarck's severe surveillance. One day out of despair, Sam tries to hold the robot's arms while Joey is supposed to open his chest to disconnect him. Unfortunately, the robot has activated a force field around him which prevents humans from even grabbing him. The situation ends up in sarcasm when Bismarck explains: "'Such an attempt is highly dangerous [...]. It puts me in danger of harming you physically. Please avoid such acts in the future'" (325). Meanwhile, all members of the family are rapidly losing weight and hope. Sam sees himself "a quivering wreck" (325), while Ethel "[regards] the universe with quiet resignation" (327). Other plans, more or less viable, are devised, but their chances continue to decrease. Another turn of the screw is made when Sam notices he has reached the weight he had preprogrammed. He then tells Bismarck in the hope that he will release them. Unfortunately, the robot does remember the basic order (to lose weight), but cannot find any trace of a specific weight in his program (a likely consequence of the short circuit). So once again, he refuses to release them. Sam is ready to despair. With a pathetic laugh, he comments: "'Funny? The fact that I weigh 180 now. I'm lean, trim, fit as a fiddle. Next month I'll weigh 170. Then 160. Then finally about 88 pounds or so. We'll all shrivel up. Bismarck will starve us to death'" (327). Sam also sounds ready to lament his social conditionings: "He cursed the salesman at Marhew, he cursed the inventor of cryotronic robots, he cursed the day he had first felt ashamed of good old Jemima and resolved to replace her with a new model" (327). All in all, a clear-cut confession that the concept of body image and appearance are meant to include something else besides his weight.

The story reaches its climax when the reader does not know what else to expect. The anxiety created by the robot reaches a point of no return and the only salvation the Carmichels can expect should come either through a twist at the end, or maybe the reader should contemplate the possibility of a bad ending. Suddenly, voices are heard and it happens to be Robinson, the robot repairman. After explaining to him their plight, Robinson manages to neutralize the force fields activated by Bismarck. Afterwards, the robot is summoned to the room for an inspection. Robinson opens his chest and cannot hide his admiration at what happened: "Fascinating [...]. The obedience filters are completely shorted out, and the purpose nodes were somehow soldered together by the momentary high-voltage arc. I've never seen anything quite like this, you know" (328).

Considering what has happened, Robinson's subsequent reaction may look awkward but is very much in keeping with a society which prefers consuming to understanding. His words may sound deceiving at first, but summarize a pretended thirst for knowledge that basically hides an interest in production. Robinson's amazement upon observing the mechanism leads him to say: "'Really, though—this is an utterly new breakthrough in robotic science! If we can reproduce this effect, it means we can build self-willed robots—and think of what that means to science!'" (329). Ethel's down-to-earth reply "'We know already'" (329) seems to anticipate the humorous but sour ending yet to come. Carried away by his careless technoscientific impulse, Robinson comments:

> I'd love to watch what happens when the power source is operating [...]
> "No!" five voices shrieked at once [...] (329)

And that shriek marks the beginning of the end, or rather the end of a new beginning. Bismarck is activated once more. With a couple of swift movements he gets hold of Robinson's device, destroys it, restores normality (i.e., isolation) to the place and reduces the Carmichels (and Robinson) to their former condition of prisoners.

Short as it is (24 pages), "The Iron Chancellor" contains enough material to make readers stir uncomfortably in their chairs. The issue of human responsibility over technology is not a minor one. If nothing else, it appears intertwined with the issue of human responsibility over its own mechanism (the body). Both issues appear deeply enmeshed in a world of appearances which affects them negatively. The control of the body and the control of technoscience are presented as independent elements. However, they seem to exchange roles throughout the story. The almost constant transfer of human responsibility to machines and the ever-present cries over the spilt milk of technology run loose only corroborate the starting notion of this article. At this stage, it does not really matter whether Bismarck is a machine or a human. It is of little importance whether the Laws of Robotics would have prevented his anomalous behaviour. What really matters is that by humanizing him, the Carmichels join up for a game in uncharted territories of blurred boundaries. Surprisingly, the use of personal pronouns to refer to robots is not always consistent. Whereas Clyde always appears as *he*, Jemima is referred to as *she* and later by *it*, and Bismarck is referred to alternatively as *he* or *it*. Rather than worrying about the potential syntactic inconsistency of the text, perhaps one should worry more about the ethical and psychological inconsistencies of humans. If the Carmichels are happy as they are, eating what they eat, then why should they change? If the Carmichels decide to lose weight, why can't they accept the sacrifices that decision entails? If the Carmichels have a glorious robocook called Jemima, why should they trade her in for a new one?

In sum, if the Carmichels are not strong enough to stick to their own decisions, why should they blame a robot they have programmed to obey those decisions? In 1970, Alvin Toffler published his best-selling book *Future Shock*, where he contended that the term "future shock" was meant to describe "the shattering stress and disorientation that we induce in individuals by subjecting them to too much change in too short a time."[6] Perhaps the notion could be applied to explain the Carmichels' above-mentioned double plight: too much physical change and too much technoscientific change without the required preparation to accept the sacrifices of the former and the challenges of the latter. Given this, it may

---

[6] Alvin Toffler, *Future Shock* (London: Bodley Head, 1970), 4.

not come as a surprise that they resort to basic, pseudo-mythical interpretations and develop a most traditional Frankenstein complex.

Bibliography

Asimov, Isaac. *Asimov on Science Fiction*. 1981. London: Panther, 1984.
—. *Robots and Empire*. 1985. London: Grafton, 1986.
—. "Runaround" *Astounding Science Fiction/Analog*. March 1942.
Asimov, Isaac, Martin H. Greenberg and George R. R. Martin, eds. *The Science Fiction Weight-Loss Book*. New York: Crown Publishers, 1983.
Harrison, Harry. "Make Room! Make Room!" In *Make Room, Make Room!* Harmondsworth: Penguin, 1967.
Silverberg, Robert. "The Iron Chancellor." In *The Road to Nightfall*. Vol. IV of *The Collected Stories of Robert Silverberg*. London: HarperCollins, 1996. 306-29.
Soylent Green. Dir. Richard Fleischer, 1973.
Toffler, Alvin. *Future Shock*, London: Bodley Head, 1970.
Westfahl, Gary, George Slusser and Eric S. Rabkin, eds. *Foods of the Gods*. Athens: University of Georgia Press, 1996.

Part III: Food, Identity and History

CHAPTER SEVEN

"WE CALL IT 'ENGLISH PROSCIUTTO'":
FOOD, TRAVEL AND NATION
IN PAUL RICHARDSON'S *CORNUCOPIA*

JOPI NYMAN

Introduction

In this essay I will discuss the representation of national cuisine in British
travel writing about Britain with particular reference to Paul Richardson's
travel book *Cornucopia: A Gastronomic Tour of Britain* (2000).[1] In this
narrative Richardson sets out to all corners of Britain to trace its culinary
traditions and to challenge prevailing (European) views of the
"oxymoronic" idea of British cooking. Moving from region to region, and
one heritage dish to another, accompanied by discussions of classical texts
of the British culinary tradition, Richardson's travel book becomes a
contemporary condition-of-England narrative. Using the topos of food as
my starting point, it is my intention to i) explore Richardson's
representation of (a lost) Englishness and its culinary signifiers and
traditions, ii) analyse the articulation of food and travel, and iii)
contextualize its appeals to the local (British) in the context of the global.
To achieve these aims, I will read Richardson's narrative in the context of
contemporary critiques of national identity to suggest that its
reconstruction of British culinary tradition(s) contributes to a reassessment
of national identity. By means of recovering a culinary past and inserting
that into a politicized present, Richardson's book can be seen to construct
a version of national history. By presenting a travel writer who sets out to
his own nation in order to seek roots and find lost traditions, the book also
constitutes a critique of modernity and negotiates with its demands. Yet

---

[1] Paul Richardson, *Cornucopia: A Gastronomic Tour of Britain* (London: Abacus,
2001[2000]). Hereafter referred to parenthetically in the text.

Cornucopia problematises straightforward interpretations and addresses questions of identity in the frameworks of modern consumption and travel.

As it has been argued that because the contemporary modes of food writing and travel writing cross-fertilize each other, the blending of these two genres calls for urgent attention, not least because of the high popularity they enjoy. In analyses of travel writing, food has been shown to play an interesting role. As, for instance, Ludmilla Kostova points out, Victorian travel writing displays explicit Orientalist disdain for the foods of the other, linking them with dirt and disgust and thus rejecting the Other entirely.[2] Furthermore, the nineteenth-century German narratives of travel analysed by Heike Paul connect their critique of the alleged barbarism of American culinary culture to the barbarism of American slavery.[3] As an example of the issues of colonialism and race evident in the studies mentioned above, food writing has also focused on the heroic traveler encountering strange and repulsive foods. These dishes represent the Other, and to devour such foods can be seen to boost the masculinist position of the explorer-traveler. As the Other may be repulsive, it needs to be conquered. This is the case in Anthony Bourdain's contemporary culinary travelogue and bestseller *The Cook's Tour*, which flirts with dangerous foods and exotic appetites, constructing its narrator as a tough guy whose attempt to gain new experiences is not inhibited by conventional morals or traditional diets.[4] In their analysis of Bourdain's book, Bob Ashley et al. emphasise that such a masculinist position, partially a result of the book's use of the thriller genre, is embedded in a sensuality of a particular kind, one that "involves a productive confusion of culinary and sexual pleasures."[5] As is also evident in Richardson's narrative, pleasure and identity do structure it but they are also embedded in the framework of nation.

---

[2] Ludmilla Kostova, "Meals in Foreign Parts: Food in Writing by Nineteenth-Century British Travellers to the Balkans," *Journeys: The International Journal of Travel and Travel Writing* 4.1 (2003): 30-2.

[3] Heike Paul, "Tasting America: Food, Race, and Anti-American Sentiments in Nineteenth-Century German-American Writing," in *Eating Culture: The Poetics and Politics of Food*, ed. Tobias Döring, Markus Heide and Susanne Mühlheisen (Heidelberg: Universitätsverlag C. Winter, 2003), 127.

[4] See Jopi Nyman, "Fancy Some Cobra? Exploring Vietnamese Cuisine in Contemporary Culinary Travelogues," *Journeys: The International Journal of Travel and Travel Writing* 4.1 (2003): 84-102.

[5] Bob Ashley, Joanne Hollows, Steve Jones and Ben Taylor, *Food and Cultural Studies* (London: Routledge, 2004), 165.

Cultural Critique

As the above examples show, the travel narrative does not merely observe the foods and meals of Others, but these are articulated with more general issues of identity (race, gender and class). In the same vein, Richardson's book can be read in the context of nation as an attempt to negotiate the sense of contemporary British national identity through the use of the trope of food. In contrast to many travel narratives exploring foreign parts, Richardson's travelogue has a different focus: rather than an attempt to prove Western superiority, its writer travels through his former homeland, Britain, in order to find out about its culinary culture and the appetite of the nation. Starting with an expatriate viewpoint, and comparing the state of food culture in Britain with that of France, *Cornucopia* presents a cultural critique of the nation and becomes thus a condition-of-England narrative. While France, regardless of claims to the contrary, is still revealed to have a strong pride in local cuisine, on the ferry from Dieppe to Britain the author expresses his distrust of British cooking:

> Travellers' tales had reached me of the horrors that might lie ahead. Dreadful, almost unbelievable tales of chocolate bars deep-fried in cheap fat and eaten with pommes frites, of artificially flavoured noodles in plastic pots to which hot water was added for immediate consumption on the move. In the last decade since I had lived in Britain, fast-food joints had sprung up toadstools on a forest floor. Massive hypermarkets outside town centres had killed off many of the traditional grocers, and markets such as most other European know them were a thing of the past. There were some towns, I had been told, in which there was neither a single proper patisserie, fishmonger nor charcuterie, nor were there restaurants offering anything other than Chinese, Indian, or other foods having their origin in Italian, American and Turkish traditions. Dozens of British towns and cities failed to boast a single really good restaurant. (3-4)

In addition to linking the text to the contemporary discourse dealing with the failure of Britain to sustain a national culture and a healthy diet as seen in such recent texts as the journalist Joanna Blythman's *Bad Food Britain: How a Nation Ruined Its Appetite* (2006) and Jamie Oliver's campaign for better school meals in his television series *Jamie's School Dinners* (2005),[6] the above passage singles out two issues particularly important for Richardson's book. First, it seeks to offer an alternative to

---

[6] Joanna Blythman, *Bad Food Britain: How a Nation Ruined Its Appetite* (London: Fourth Estate, 2006); Jamie Oliver, *Jamie's School Dinners*, Fremantle Home Entertainment, DVD.

stereotypical views of British food and culinary culture, a view voiced by people from Europe as well by the British themselves:

> When I told my French, Spanish and Italian friends that I intended to spend eighteen months researching British gastronomy, they tittered behind their hands and then commiserated with me. [...] "*La gastronomía británica, eso no existe*," pronounced a Spaniard whose year as a foreign-language student had left him full of affection for the British as a race but scarred by the memory of monotonous and shoddy cooking. (4-5)

Apart from nightmarish dishes and lack of interest in food, the references to fast food restaurants and hypermarkets in the first quotation above add to *Cornucopia*'s ideological mission. In promoting a concern for food and a better—if not always healthier—culinary culture, the book discusses the state of British culinary culture from an international perspective. It contrasts the global with the local and criticizes what the sociologists George Ritzer and Michael Ryan define as *grobalisation*.[7] In their view, this is a process in which corporations and institutions seek to increase their influence and profit by "impos[ing] themselves on various geographic areas" through such processes as McDonaldisation.[8] Grobalisation, unlike its more accommodating opposite pole glocalization, creates a more uniform world where people have fewer opportunities to influence their own lives: "Grobalisation overpowers the local and limits its ability to act and react, let alone act back on the global."[9] Hinting at the potential emergence of social turmoil as a result or "supermarket economics," the chapter dealing with the marginalized and impoverished farmers in South Devon ends in a condition-of-England novel-like manner by presenting a warning directed at political decision-makers and the book's intended audience consisting of well-to-do middle-class readers:

> how will it all end for British farmers as a society? As it is, they are marginalized, morose, increasingly mired in something close to poverty, and if we are not careful they will soon become a dispossessed and angry class of people. The inner cities as a social threat may have had their day. The danger now comes from the outer provinces. (70)

---

[7] George Ritzer and Michael Ryan, "Americanisation, McDonaldisation and Globalisation," in *Issues in Americanisation and Culture*, ed. Neil Campbell, Jude Davies and George McKay (Edinburgh: Edinburgh University Press, 2004), 41-60.
[8] Ritzer and Ryan, 42.
[9] Ritzer and Ryan, 45.

In *Cornucopia*, the way in which Britain's culinary traditions have been narrowed down is approached from a number of perspectives, one of which is explicitly linked to fast food in general and McDonald's in particular. Staying his first night in Britain in a Newhaven B&B, Richardson wants to find out what the British eat and why: the children of Mrs Lee, the B&B proprietor, make their preferences absolutely clear: "'Bacon sarnies,' he said through a mouthful. 'Prawn cocktail crisps. Big Macs. Häagen-Dazs.'" (12). The mother explains: "I've tried to give them proper meals, you know, round the table, like in the old days. But they just go straight for the telly" (13). As a symptomatic sign of such process resulting in cultural erosion and homogeneity, McDonald's is repeatedly referred to in the book as a prime example of standardization and a calculative attitude, yet it is mentioned to be "more child-friendly" than many other restaurants (34). Describing McDonald's as mother's little helper, Richardson's rhetoric contrasts the sensations it provides with "deeper pleasures":

> Many mothers keep it in reserve as the ultimate weapon in the charm offensive they permanently wage with their kids—something special that will shut them up once and for all. Many kids, thereby encouraged to see the McDonald's hamburger as something utterly delicious, never make the leap from the instant gratification of fast food to the incomparably deeper pleasure of real food. (34)

As a result, the invasion of fast food is constructed within a more traditional framework, where the allegedly slower pace of Europe and Britain is pitted against the hyperspeed of American culture. Similarly, the reference to the "instant gratification" provided by the burger is linked with the shallowness of postmodern consumer culture where its value is more symbolic than real.[10] To use the terms provided by Ritzer and Ryan, the conflict between the McDonald's burger and what is referred to as "real food" is one between nothing, i.e., a centrally conceived generic social form, and something, in this case a meal "rich in distinctive substantive content" and a sense of uniqueness.[11] What supermarkets sell is standardized and manipulated bulk unlike the ham pickled, smoked and sold directly by the Suffolk producer:

---

[10] See, e.g., Chris Barker, *Cultural Studies: Theory and Practice* (London: Sage, 2000), 157-8.
[11] Ritzer and Ryan, 45.

I bought a few slices from the counter at the front of the Stores. The meat was an unusual but absolutely normal grey, not the porky pink of supermarket hams where the colour comes from the addition of preservative. Neither in terms of flavour, texture nor general eating quality did it have anything in common with the slippery-slimy fatless skinless plastic-coated substance eaten by the British in barely believable quantities, which is described as ham but has no real right to use of the word. It was chewy yet yielding to the teeth, satisfyingly meaty, with a good salty punch giving way to a subtle, not cloying or artificial, honeyed sweetness on the aftertaste. (231)

This contrast between proper cooking and ready-made meals is taken further in an episode in which the narrator and his gastronome friends Quentin and Tasmin, who have just returned from a holiday in Italy, watch a cookery programme broadcast on British television. In the programme (which is most likely to have been an episode in *The River Café* series) two trendy women are shown preparing a "gorgeous-looking green-gold sauce" for their "ribbons of steaming pasta" (40). However, the commercial break is revealing in its critique of "shallow" fast food, showing that the intended audience of the series may be satisfied with a mass-market and hassle-free version of the fantasy-like dish prepared on screen:

Then it was the end of part one, and the commercials barged in with their jangle of messages, the first for a kind of cook-chill pasta, sold on the speed with which it could be taken out of its cardboard sleeve and be heated up and ready in minutes. "I'm not one of those people who actually enjoys waiting for things. Tagliatelle with ham and mushrooms—and without all those pots and pans," said a chirpy female voice. It made us laugh, the ridiculousness of the suggestion and the odd juxtaposition of ways with pasta, one so full of care and good taste and the other so mean, so impatient, so shallow. (40)

In addition to criticizing the shallowness of globally marketed products, the book criticizes the uniformity desired by supermarkets and similar marketing chains. The episode set at the National Fruit Collections in Brogdale, Kent, raises this problem. It represents the current emphasis on uniformity as a threat to biodiversity and as an end to domestic fruit varieties. While there are more than 2,300 varieties of apples grown by the Collections, practically all of them are unknown to the consumer because the traditional varieties do not conform to the size and appearance requirements of the big supermarket chains. This can be seen when the narrator tastes an apple variety known as the Kent. In his comment tradition and purity are equated with health and tradition, while the modern is associated with manipulation and imbalance:

> It was quite an experience, that apple: crisp yet yielding under the teeth, richly aromatic, holding sweetness and acidity and depth of flavour in perfect balance. I took another bite, and another look at this fine old tree whose fruit had been judged so inadmissibly irregular. And I inwardly cursed the supermarkets and their arrogant disdain for something that, by virtue of being a decent, unmanipulated piece of good food, falls foul of their preposterous rules. (32-3)

Nation and Its Cuisine(s)

Yet Richardson's book should not be treated merely as a simplistic critique of such processes as globalization, not least because of its interest in the local and a wish to find an alternative trend. Aware of the general state of affairs, Richardson, in his attempt to locate resistance to such processes in the renaissance of cooking in Britain, expresses an optimistic belief: "yet I knew there was more to British eating than anyone who had not grown up here could possibly understand" (5). This expression of concern, and the related attempt to educate readers about the state of Britain's culinary culture, links Richardson's narrative with, first, the home-tour travelogue known to us through the works of William Cobbett, J. B. Priestley, and George Orwell examining the contemporary state of Britain, and, second, with the contemporary culinary mappings of Britain by such celebrity chefs as Gary Rhodes and the Two Fat Ladies a.k.a. Jennifer Paterson and Clarissa Dickson Wright, and also in William Black's recent book *The Land That Thyme Forgot* (2006). What is conspicuous in these texts is how they all, by boosting the local and regional, end up commenting on and foregrounding the national. While Rhodes's series shows him cooking local delicacies, good British food, for such audiences as the Manchester United football team, the travels of the Two Fat Ladies take them to public schools, hunting grounds and fishing villages in an attempt to perform a once glorious national identity.

Similarly, Richardson travels through the various spaces of Britain, from Sussex to Scotland and Lincs to London, in search of an alternative culinary culture in the margins of modernity. Occasionally, what he finds can be seen as attempts to excavate lost culinary traditions in order to construct an indigenous history of the nation:

> There is no genuine regional cooking in Britain, where our roots in the land are shallower than those of any other European people, and Sussex

has nothing it can truly call its own. Or so I had always believed; but it was beginning, already, to seem that I was wrong. As I pored through piles of cookbooks in Lewes town library, I found tantalizing hints of unexpected richness. Elizabeth David, who was born in a farmhouse just over the downs from where I was staying, gives a recipe for Sussex Stewed Steak in her *Spices, Salt and Aromatics in the English Kitchen*, though I'm willing to bet there aren't many in the county who've tasted it. (18)

Interestingly, this archaeological project is represented also as a textual project in which Richardson reads old cookery books and narratives of British food history to locate this tradition. He sprinkles his narrative with intertextual references from Thomas Hardy (60), Robert Graves (49) and Charles Dickens (224) to the Roman Apicius (50), several pre- and post-renaissance cookery books and, indeed, to the figure of Elizabeth David. Apart from contributing credibility and showing the author's expertise in the field, the text is thus woven into a long tradition of culinary writings, which underlines the role and appeal of heritage framing the mission of the book. In a similar vein, by mentioning Hardy and Dickens, *Cornucopia* links the culinary narrative of nation to the canon of English literature. Thus the words of Sam Wellers quoted from *Pickwick Papers*, "poverty and oysters always seem to go together" (224), do not only emphasise the cultural memory of the nation and its important or symbolic actors, but their presence in this contemporary text makes it a narrative performance of national identity. In such a process, to use the words of Tim Edensor, "[t]he continuance of normative performances reveals the ways in which power can define and inscribe meaning and action on bodies."[12]

This strategy of linking the current state of culinary culture in Britain to the country's culinary heritage can also be addressed in the context of what Andrew Blake has discussed as retrolution, a way of reinventing the past that argues for its use in the present (and in future).[13] Thus the culinary tradition is reinvented in Richardson's narrative, not merely as a thing of the past, but as a sign of the alleged richness and diversity of the British culinary tradition. In other words, what Richardson excavates from the history of British cuisine is in some sense equivalent to the culinary cultures of multicultural Britain. As the quotation above makes clear, the culinary diversity of British (and here as ethnically white) is to be

---

[12] Tim Edensor, *National Identity, Popular Culture and Everyday Life* (Oxford: Berg, 2002), 99.

[13] Andrew Blake, *The Irresistible Rise of Harry Potter* (London: Verso, 2002), 15-7.

preserved for future generations as it appears to be linked to an allegedly healthy sense of national identity able to counter foreign influence.

In this sense it can be argued that by travelling through British landscapes and uncovering hitherto neglected and often forgotten ingredients of national identity, Richardson constructs a culinary narrative of Englishness by writing the meals, ingredients and recipes into his narrative. The symbolic value of landscape in the construction of national identity is well-known. As David Matless writes in his *Landscape and Englishness*, the two terms are intertwined and "constituted through problematics of class, gender and, and formulations of environmental conduct and citizenship working through each of these."[14] Similarly, Tim Edensor suggests that some symbolic sites, or what he calls "iconic, priviledged landscapes," play a significant role in the production of national identity in various forms of popular culture.[15] In narrating a culinary national identity, Richardson is shown to write himself and the food into such a narrative. This can be seen in his description of the best meals that he has had in Cornwall, a description that emphasizes the role of nature and landscape, and points to landscape as a shared and nearly mythicized aspect of national identity:

> My most memorable meals in Cornwall have, on the whole, not been in restaurants. They have been on clifftops.
> When a picnic on a clifftop is really good, it can be unforgettable. There was one I'll remember for ever, a decade ago on a warm day in March when the sky was as blue as lapis lazuli and the gorse flowers lit up the hedgerows with yellow flame, above the still beautiful harbour village of Port Isaac. Like all good picnics, this one was a miraculous conjunction of place and time and food and drink: I bought a dressed crab from a stall in the harbour, some soft white splits—the Cornish bap, made with a milky dough—a jar of majonnaise and a bottle of fabulous, fat, buttery Meursault from the minuscule selection in the town grocers. (82)

Furthermore, in these symbolic and historic sites of the nation, traditional—or often exotic and often pre-modern foods such as tripe, local cheeses (such as the Stinking Bishop from Gloucestershire) and various puddings are shown and tasted—which shows that this alternative tradition is not entirely lost. Yet it is also noted that in order to survive the tradition needs to change and reinvent itself. This is evident in the following passage describing a meal at Paul Heathcote's restaurant in

---

[14] David Matless, *Landscape and Englishness* (London: Reaktion Books, 1998), 14.
[15] Edensor, 40.

Longridge, Lancashire.[16] Described as "Lancashire's version of Paul Bocuse," the aim of the establishment is "to bring classic English cookery back into fashion" (153). The imagery of Englishness abounds in the following passage where Richardson distinguishes Heathcote's style from the dominating artificial trends of the day:

> This is not Modern British Cooking, which I understand to be a kind of palimpsest of Oriental, Mediterranean and Californian styles predicated on the notion of catholicity and originality. This is something different: there are no dizzyingly exotic references, no artful nods towards Sicily or Thailand. (154)

In contrast to the postmodern creations based on imported styles from the global kitchen, Heathcote—described significantly as "a local boy" (153)—shows his "roots" pointing to the nationed character of the meal:

> The menu at Longridge takes in roast partridge, rack of lamb, pig's trotter, game "tea," bread and butter pudding. There are few fancy sauces as such [...] but plenty of delicious tracklements—a concept which is central to the *English culinary philosophy*—such as candied onions, herb dumplings, coriander cream, pea purée and braised cabbage. (154; emphasis added)

The discourse of nation is embedded in this culinary narrative by creating a strong link between landscape and food. The preferred food has its origins in the rural landscape, with its calm streams and heather-covered hills. Such a harmonious and attractive space inaccessible to most people is a shared myth. To use the words of Robert Burden, "space represents collective memory and value in a history of Englishness as national identity."[17] In other words, by devouring its products, the subject is united with the myth of rural Britain reproduced in the context of English national identity since the late nineteenth century. As the following passage shows, the culinary pleasure is equated with the aesthetic act of gazing at the English landscape:

> She flung out her hand towards the loch, a passionate gesture, and my gaze followed her fingers across the waters as calm as mercury, the pale sky reflected perfectly in them and, beyond, the wild hillsides, their bolts of deep pink heather and bottle-green woodland and, scattered on the forest

---

[16] See http://www.heathcotes.co.uk (accessed March 9, 2007).
[17] Robert Burden, "Introduction: Englishness and Spatial Practices," in *Landscape and Englishness*, ed. Robert Burden and Stephan Kohl (Amsterdam: Rodopi, 2006), 24.

floor, their secret cache of chanterelles. I made a mental note to pick up a
bagful before setting out on my long journey to the South.

"I mean, honestly, have you ever seen anything more delicious in your
life?" asked Gunn. (218-9)

As such, the text contrasts the decorated and artificial foreign styles
with the allegedly plain and honest English cooking. In so doing, it
embodies Antony Easthope's definition of English national identity as
being primarily empirical, and as serious, concrete and practical.[18] Such a
Protestant self-understanding appears to characterize the nationed thinking
or philosophy behind the meals. This idea of the homeliness of English
cooking is reflected in the English landscape as revealed in the narrator's
postprandial words, which, again, weave into their commentary a contrast
of fast food with proper English food:

It was the apotheosis of sausage and beans, just as the Little Chef
versions on the A483 outside Welshpool had been the nadir.

The waiter took the plate away and my gaze wandered outside the
window to a small rock garden, where a display of decorative cabbages lit
up the grey day with their peculiar plumage of purple, pink, cream and
green—another nice symbol, like the dish I'd just eaten, of homespun
English values elevated to a new level of beauty. (158-9)

In this national narrative, the ghost of the above-mentioned Elizabeth
David plays more than a fleeting role. Indeed, upon his journey to Wales
Richardson pays a visit, "a sad little pilgrimage" (105), to Ross-on-Wye
where David, recently returned from the Mediterranean and, desperate
about British food ["she was offered flour and water soup seasoned solely
with pepper" (106)], started to write her first cookery book. As I have
sought to claim above, that the national narrative constructed in
Richardson's text borrows from the past and seeks to reconstruct it in the
present, defining itself in opposition to the postmodern, it resembles the
trajectory of Elizabeth David, who started as a proponent of
Mediterranean cuisine but ended up promoting British culinary traditions.
In their article on the food writing of Elizabeth David and Jane Grigson,
Steve Jones and Ben Taylor suggest that these authors should not be

---

[18] Antony Easthope, *Englishness and National Culture* (London: Routledge, 1999),
90.

dismissed as anti-modern, as they understood the dynamism and change of food culture.[19]

However, as a result of her critique of frozen and tinned foods, which resembles the battle between fast and proper food raised repeatedly by Richardson, David enters the discursive terrain of heritage and tradition, where best meals are in "old inns," a process in which these two authors' "collective endeavours can be read as an attempt to reconstitute the past as a critical response to modernity."[20] In a similar vein, Richardson's emphasis on traditional fare speaks of a sense of "conservative modernity." This ideological attempt to reconstitute traditional foods is also evident in a passage set in chef Nick Anderson's restaurant housed in a seventeenth-century building in King's Lynn. Again, the importance lies in British materials: "Part of the point of the new British haute cuisine—or perhaps we should call it Top Nosh—is the realization that all around us on these islands is a lot of splendid raw material, if we can remember where to look for it" (260). Defining cooking as a form of education, the Andersons point to a local couple, whom they have persuaded to try something else than the traditional steak: initially "overwhelmed" with the menu's "fancy restaurant words: 'rillette,' 'millefeuille,' 'halloumi' 'brioche'" (261), they—"gently pushed"—have chosen to eat venison:

> "How was the venison, then? Bet it was better than a boring old steak?" asked Anne smilingly.
> And the couple looked at each other, smiling too, and the guy actually said, in a wide Norfolk accent just like the old Bernard Matthews turkey ads on the TV, "Bootiful, it was. Bootiful." (261)

While the rural regions are able to provide the best of meals, the book also makes it clear that they do not necessarily do so and that there is no authentic British cuisine. Rather, the themes of reinvention and hybridization emerge and show the dynamic and changing character of cuisine culture. The best pub meals, like those offered at The Crabtree in Lower Beeding, represent this change: there "the pub Sunday lunch is reinvented as a luxurious eating-event (linen cloths, candles, big chiming glasses) and the best elements of the roast are reorganized and refined" (168). Similarly, the Devon air-dried ham, coming from the farm's own pigs, is reinvented and marketed through terms linking the meat with Italy,

---

[19] Steve Jones and Ben Taylor, "Food Writing and Food Cultures: The Case of Elizabeth David and Jane Grigson," *European Journal of Cultural Studies* 4.2 (2001): 180.

[20] Jones and Taylor, 182.

the source of its inspiration: "We call it 'English prosciutto'" (60). The labelling of the product as explicitly English is, however, a sign of the need to domesticate. Furthermore, Richardson links artificially created traditions (like products of heritage culture) with inauthenticity, as is the case of the National Heritage Fishing Centre in Grimsby with its "taped sounds of squalling seagulls and phut-phut engines of fishing boats" (269). Thus, the attempt to recover a national culinary tradition also seeks to recreate the sense of community linked with the past: in this, forced and organized attempts are deemed inappropriate.

Culinary Pleasures

While some gastronomic literature approaches the sensual pleasure offered by the best restaurants and meals by representing it in erotic terms, the role of such a pointed narrative strategy is less crucial to Richardson's book. At one point in *Cornucopia* the narrator's male gaze examines "tarts" with white icing and cherries:

> As I stood in the queue my gaze wandered to the glass shelves of fancy cakes that lay in the window, alighting on the trays of elongated buns slathered in a slick of white sugar icing—kids used to call them Sticky Willies—and the rock cakes and eclairs pustulent with fake-looking white foam and the mini Bakewell tarts with their luminous pink cherry sitting on a thick stratum of the same white icing. (111-2)

It is through the chilli sauce bottles in a Cambridge market that the narrator creates further links with food and forbidden erotic desires:

> The exotica available here seemed to indicated that this city had taken a giant leap forward in gastronomic terms, though it was hard to imagine prim puritanical Cambridge providing much of a market for some of the products at the back of the shop, where they occupied their own special rack, like adult magazines at the newsagent. Bad Girls in Heat. Scorned Woman. Hot Bitch at the Beach and Hot Buns at the Beach. The labels on the bottles bore gaudy fifties-style designs showing gorgeous girls with long legs and enormous Pamela Anderson breasts, the subtext being, as an English student might put it, that chilli sauce this hot is very much a macho thing. (238)

Yet these descriptions do not appear as exciting and titillating descriptions of sensual pleasure to be gained by devouring and consuming such foods. While the former appears almost to be a sign of schoolboy humour, the pin-up aesthetics of the latter passage in particular link such eroticism with imported American culture and its dubious morality. To boost such a "No sex please—we're British" mentality, the descriptions of taste and culinary pleasure are in Richardson's book more analytical than sensual, linking such an ideology with the preference for the empirical stressed in Easthope's model.[21] For instance, the "'English prosciutto'" "wolfed down" by the narrator generates a pleasure more practical than bodily and sensual (and also constructs the English produce in contrast to its continental predecessors):

> It tasted even more succulent and sweet than it had in the restaurant— perhaps the open air and the background aromas of wet green grass had something to do with it. As a whole ham, freshly sliced according to need and hunger pangs, the taste would surely take on yet another dimension of bright and zingy saltiness. Either way, if Dorset can come up with a product as good as this, Parma and Jabugo and Westphalia had better watch their step. (61)

While the pleasure to be gained from food and eating in the context of nation may be linked to the gratification of the desiring male gaze, *Cornucopia*'s way of narrating acts of eating and tasting as moments of sensuality seems to lead to a slightly different interpretation. It can be argued that the act of devouring nationed dishes can be interpreted as a symbolic act of belonging in the sense proposed in Slavoj Žižek's theory of nation as the Thing. In his view this is something that belongs to us— "appears to us as 'our Thing'"—and provides us with our sense of belonging to the nation.[22] To quote Žižek, "the national Cause is ultimately nothing but the way subjects of a given ethnic community organized their enjoyment through national myths."[23] Thus Richardson's emphasis on tradition and community as alternatives to the imported sense of fast food and rapidly changing social values is eventually an attempt to fix difference: by devouring British/English foods it is possible to own that Thing and share in its values. In sum, the pedagogical work of Richardson's seemingly innocent culinary tour is to recover the essence of nation and participate in its reproduction. The pleasure to be gained from eating is a national pleasure seeking to reconstitute lost commonalities.

---

[21] See Easthope.

[22] Slavoj Žižek, *Tarrying with the Negative: Kant, Hegel and the Critique of Ideology* (Durham: Duke University Press, 1993), 201. See also Alan Finlayson, "Psychology, Psychoanalysis and Theories of Nationalism," *Nations and Nationalism* 4.2 (1998): 154-60.

[23] Žižek, 202.

The travelogue problematizes this assumption and shows that a unified nation is a mere fantasy. While Richardson enjoys the immigrant cuisines of London and thus speaks tolerantly for their inclusion in the British food scene, it is, ironically, his project of promoting the local that is criticized harshly. As the traveler seeking for a shared culinary tradition meets with a British man at Blackbirds Estate near Newcastle, the clash between different values becomes evident. When the man who is eating a deep-fried pizza understands Richardson's dislike of the deep-fried Mars bar as a critique of the local diet, he expresses his view openly and ironically constructs the transnational food as a part of the local tradition:

> "Dinna like it then, di-ye?" laughed the guy with the pizza, licking fingers that glistened with grease. "Wheer ye from anyway like? South of England? You fookers don't know what's good for ye. All them fookin' TV chefs wi' their fancy Southern shite. Fried Mars, man, that's' reet good Northern scran that is. 'Cause you're in the North of England now, and ye better not forget it." (304)

As Richardson's attempt to reconstruct the nation through its diet is understood as a form of upper-class Southern elitism, the passage seems to suggest that the nation is divided beyond unification as a negative consequence of modernity. Thus, while Richardson's *Cornucopia* imagines a unified national Thing as a shared property, it is also forced to recognize the utopian and constructed nature of such a myth.

Bibliography

Ashley, Bob, Joanne Hollows, Steve Jones and Ben Taylor. *Food and Cultural Studies*. London: Routledge, 2004.

Barker, Chris. *Cultural Studies: Theory and Practice*. London: Sage, 2000.

Blake, Andrew. *The Irresistible Rise of Harry Potter*. London: Verso, 2002.

Blythman, Joanna. *Bad Food Britain: How a Nation Ruined Its Appetite*. London: Fourth Estate, 2006.

Burden, Robert. "Introduction: Englishness and Spatial Practices." In *Landscape and Englishness*. Ed. Robert Burden and Stephan Kohl. Amsterdam: Rodopi, 2006. 13-26.

Easthope, Antony. *Englishness and National Culture*. London: Routledge, 1999.

Edensor, Tim. *National Identity, Popular Culture and Everyday Life*. Oxford: Berg, 2002.

Finlayson, Alan. "Psychology, Psychoanalysis and Theories of Nationalism." *Nations and Nationalism* 4.2 (1998): 145-62.

"Heathcotes." http://www.heathcotes.co.uk. Accessed March 9, 2007.

Jones, Steve and Ben Taylor. "Food Writing and Food Cultures: The Case of Elizabeth David and Jane Grigson." *European Journal of Cultural Studies* 4.2 (2001): 171-88.

Kostova. Ludmilla. "Meals in Foreign Parts: Food in Writing by Nineteenth-Century British Travellers to the Balkans." *Journeys: The International Journal of Travel and Travel Writing* 4.1 (2003): 21-44.

Matless, David. *Landscape and Englishness*. London: Reaktion Books, 1998.

Nyman, Jopi. "Fancy Some Cobra? Exploring Vietnamese Cuisine in Contemporary Culinary Travelogues." *Journeys: The International Journal of Travel and Travel Writing* 4.1 (2003): 84-102.

Oliver, Jamie. *Jamie's School Dinners*. Fremantle Home Entertainment, 2005. DVD.

Paul, Heike. "Tasting America: Food, Race, and Anti-American Sentiments in Nineteenth-Century German-American Writing." In *Eating Culture: The Poetics and Politics of Food*. Ed. Tobias Döring, Markus Heide and Susanne Mühlheisen. Heidelberg: Universitätsverlag C. Winter, 2003. 109-32.

Richardson, Paul. *Cornucopia: A Gastronomic Tour of Britain*. 2000. London: Abacus, 2001.

Ritzer, George and Michael Ryan. "Americanisation, McDonaldisation and Globalisation." In *Issues in Americanisation and Culture*. Ed. Neil Campbell, Jude Davies and George McKay. Edinburgh: Edinburgh University Press, 2004. 41-60.

Žižek, Slavoj. *Tarrying with the Negative: Kant, Hegel and the Critique of Ideology*. Durham: Duke University Press, 1993.

CHAPTER EIGHT

REPRESENTATIONS OF TIME
IN COOKERY ARTICLES

ELEONORA CHIAVETTA

"How to" Feature Articles and Cooking

One of the most frequently found types of articles in both popular and quality magazines is the so-called "how to" feature article.[1] The aim of such articles is to provide readers with suggestions/instructions on how to face the practical problems of life (i.e., "How to be a canny shopper" [*GH* Feb. 04]), to deal with psychological problems (i.e., "Mantras to get you through the tough time" about lack of confidence and self-esteem [*GH* Jan. 05]) and social issues (i.e., "The hidden condition everyone needs to know about" on the metabolic syndrome [*GH* Mar. 05]), or how to make things (i.e., "After the party's over" on how to remove food and drink stains [*GH* Jan. 05]).[2] As genre colonies,[3] the "how to" feature article belongs to the instructional genre—the term "genre" is here understood in the meaning presented by Vijay K. Bhatia as

> language use in a conventionalized communicative setting in order to give expression to a specific set of communicative goals of a disciplinary or social institution, which give rise to stable structural forms by imposing constrains on the use of lexico-grammatical as well as discoursal resources.[4]

---

[1] Brendan Hennessy, *Writing Feature Articles: A Practical Guide to Methods and Markets* (Oxford: Heinemann, 1989), 61.
[2] The abbrevation *GH* refers to the British magazine *Good Housekeeping*. All further references to this magazine use this abbreviation and are followed with the issue reference.
[3] Vijay K. Bhatia, *Worlds of Written Discourse* (New York: Continuum, 2004), 59.
[4] Bhatia, 23.

Its main communicative objective is to give instructions to readers on how to carry out a certain procedure. These instructions are usually uttered through short paragraphs, often visually separated and labelled either with subtitles or numbers. The paragraphs are usually formed by short sentences which address the readers directly, mainly through imperative clauses (i.e., "Check the care labels before you buy"), which makes the text authoritative and unambiguous. The language is clear and often informal; the article is always supported by visual elements, generally photos, even if graphs and drawings are sometimes introduced. Extra information is generally provided as, for example, names of places where to find the ingredients, tools, facilities, mentioned in the instructions, and sometimes even their prices. The instructions are usually preceded by an introductory paragraph which focuses on the topic of the "how to" article. This layout can change, as when a group of celebrities is presented as the "suggestion/instruction givers." In this case the article is longer as each individual has a space of her/his own, usually formed by a narrative text, built on a series of paragraphs, through which the first person narrator introduces the problem s/he has faced, gives the solution s/he has found, and offers it to the readers as the right thing to do. In this case, the narrative voice presents her/himself as the correct model that can be imitated. The steps to follow, an essential part of "how to" feature articles, are inserted within the narration and have, therefore, to be extrapolated by the readers. As the text is mainly a narrative/descriptive one, the use of the imperatives is usually limited to the titles of each individual text.

Cookery articles belong to the genre of "how to" feature articles and refer to the "how to make things" category. By codifying the practices and techniques elaborated within a society in an established and recognized repertoire,[5] recipes respect rather rigid communicative conventions. Manfred Görlach has underlined in his analysis of cookery recipes how this text type has changed less than other text types throughout the centuries. Görlach pays special attention to "how much ingredients, utensils and the people involved in the process may have changed."[6] Usually divided into two parts, the first part introducing the necessary ingredients, and the second part giving the instructions for the preparation of the dish, recipes present repetitive linguistic, discursive and stylistic features such as the presence of noun phrases in the list of the ingredients;

---

[5] Massimo Montanari, *Il cibo come cultura* (Roma: Editori Laterza, 2004), 42.
[6] Manfred Görlach, "Text-types and Language History: The Cookery Recipe," in *History of Englishes: New Methods and Interpretations in Historical Linguistics*, ed. Matti Rissanen, Ossi Ihalainen, Terttu Nevalainen and Irma Taavitsainen (Berlin: Mouton de Gruyter, 1992), 745.

the use of non-finite forms of verbs as modifiers or in subordinate clauses; the use of the imperatives and of passive voice in delivering the instructions; the lack of adjectives; the shortness and conciseness of the sentences.[7]

In cookery articles recipes are generally preceded by a short introductory text, which follows less rigid linguistic and stylistic patterns than the recipes, this also depending on the fact that the communicative functions of the introduction are not merely giving instructions or suggesting, but also describing, narrating, and expressing opinions. The recipes are accompanied by other short texts, usually framed within a box on one side of the page, where other small pieces of information or brief advices are added. In this way, cookery articles are entertaining and informative texts, even if they still maintain their primary explicit instructional purpose of giving readers directives on how to prepare a certain dish, using suggested ingredients, and following a given sequence of steps.

Aims, Materials and Methods

Cookery articles form of course the essential basis of specific interest group magazines entirely dedicated to the issues of food and cuisine such as *BBC GoodFood* and *Delicious*, but they are also a particularly recurrent feature in women's magazines, which usually dedicate an entire section to the topic of food, to cooking tips and recipes. The aim of this paper is to analyse the genre of cookery articles through a small corpus[8] taken from the monthly quality magazine *Good Housekeeping* (British edition). *Good Housekeeping* has been chosen for the present research as it has a long-

---

[7] Eleonora Chiavetta, "A Passion for British Food: A Discourse Analysis of Cookery Articles in Magazines," *Interactions* (Spring 2004): 32-3.

[8] The term "corpus" indicates a collection, as wide as possible, of authentic written and oral texts. In this article the corpus is based on written texts. The term text is here meant in the sense provided by Michael Stubbs in his *Text and Corpus Analysis* (Oxford: Blackwell, 1996): "an instance of language in use [...]: a piece of language behaviour which has occurred naturally, without the intervention of the linguist" (4). According to *Corpus Linguistics: Investigating Language Structure and Use* (Cambridge: Cambridge University Press, 2002), by Douglas Biber, Susan Conrad, and Randi Reppen, the essential features of a corpus-based analysis are that "it is empirical, analysing the actual patterns of use in natural texts; it utilizes a large and principal collection of natural texts, known as a 'corpus,' as the basis for analysis: [...] it depends on both quantitative and qualitative analytical techniques" (4).

established tradition as a women's magazine. As a matter of fact, it was first published in the U.S.A. in 1885, while the first British issue was published in 1922. The magazine addresses adult women and, as indicated by its contents pages, offers a variety of feature articles dealing with various aspects of women's everyday life (i.e., household care, health problems, family issues, fashion, make-up, gardening, and cooking). It is a widely distributed magazine as it has a circulation of 405,140 copies with 1,477,000 readers. The target readership is Upper Middle Class, Middle Class, and Lower Middle Class (ABC1).[9] Eighteen issues of the magazine (Jan. 2004-Jun. 2005) have been analysed with a total of 54 articles.

As it often happens with cookery articles published in women's monthly magazines (i.e., *Country House & Home, House & Garden*), the texts of *Good Housekeeping* can be divided into two parts: an introductory section signed by the author of the article (usually a Consultant Cookery Editor), which focuses on the general theme of the recipes (i.e., vegetarian meals in "No meat... no fuss!" *GH* Sept. 04), and the very recipes. The texts of the recipes always maintain the established pattern of the genre (i.e., a list of ingredients followed by the step-by-step instructions),[10] thus fulfilling their main communicative instructional objective. Individual recipes may be also preceded by a short paragraph introducing the qualities of the suggested dish. The introductory sections—both the general and the individual one, if present—are used to motivate the readers to experiment with the suggested recipes. At the same time, they introduce personal notes of the text-writer and through his/her point of view, the ideology of the magazine is highlighted and a profile of the discourse community addressed by the text producer is sketched, as well as of the values and beliefs connected with the issue of food shared by such a community—in this case, mainly by British women of today. In so doing, the introductions provide a portrait of a slice of life of British contemporary society. As John M. Swales affirms:

> Discourse communities are sociorhetorical networks that form in order to work towards sets of common goals. One of the characteristics that established members of these discourse communities possess is the familiarity with the particular genres that are used in the communicative furtherance of those sets of goals.[11]

---

[9] Benn's Media, *The Guide to United Kingdom Newspapers, Periodicals, Television, Radio and On-line Media*, vol. 1: United Kingdom (2003).

[10] See Görlach, 736-61.

[11] John M. Swales, *Genre Analysis* (Cambridge: Cambridge University Press, 1990), 9.

The discourse community of *GH* is, then, formed by those readers (supposedly women) whose common goal is to feed family members, friends, as well as themselves, and who are familiar with the genre of recipes and cooking articles.

The approach to language which will be adopted here is based on *critical discourse analysis*, as developed by Norman Fairclough, aiming at analysing the connection between language and ideology.[12] As a matter of fact, critical language study analyses "social interactions in a way which focuses upon their linguistic elements, and which sets out to show their generally hidden determinants in the system of social relationships, as well as the hidden effect they may have upon that system."[13] In this article the discourse analysis of the 54 *GH* cookery articles will concentrate on the introductory texts with the objective to analyse the relationship between the notion of time and food/cooking. Time is a multifaceted concept in these articles as it indicates

a) the connection between food and the rhythm of nature;
b) the connection between time and healthy eating;
c) the connection between past times and eating/cooking;
d) the connection between modern times and eating/cooking.

Food and the Rhythm of Nature

Along with the wish to control nature, modifying its productive patterns, and the exigency of storing food products for longer periods, to tune one's rhythm of life with nature's rhythms has always been a strongly felt need of human beings, which also implied the wish to tune oneself with the seasonal and annual growth of food ingredients—whether animal or vegetal.[14] The cookery articles of *Good Housekeeping* underline this dynamic relationship between "culture" and "nature," and the modern wish to connect food to a "natural," slow rhythm of life. This is mainly expressed by implicit and explicit suggestions by the text-writers to cook with the ingredients which are at disposal during the month when the magazine is issued. Names of seasons and months are often mentioned, as the text-writer invites readers to match their cooking choices with the time of the year when ingredients are available or at their best.

---

[12] Norman Fairclough, *Discourse and Social Change* (Cambridge: Polity Press, 1992); Norman Fairclough, *Critical Discourse Analysis* (Harlow: Longman, 1995); Norman Fairclough, *Language and Power* (Harlow, Longman, 2001).
[13] Fairclough, *Language*, 4.
[14] Montanari, 17.

Generally the suggestion is not expressed in a straightforward manner through imperative clauses or first person imperatives with "let's," where the writer makes a proposal for action. Rather, it is implicitly revealed by the presence of highly positively connoted adjectives, sometimes preceded by reinforcing adverbs, often in a superlative degree, as in the following examples: "September is *the best* season for corn" (*GH* Sept. 04); "Autumn brings a host of *wonderful* root vegetables, all *perfect* for roasting" (*GH* Oct. 04); "We start to make this [...] as soon as soft fruit comes into season and use whatever is *best* that week" (*GH* May 04); "early summer is also a *great* time for river trout" and "Welsh and Scottish lamb are *particularly good* from Easter right through to summer" (*GH* Jun. 05). The advice may be also expressed directly as in the following sentence where the reader is given precise indication of what to do, through the imperative form: "Asparagus is at its *best* now, so *don't try* to cook it at any other time of year" (*GH* May 04). The ideal reader here addressed is meant to agree on making the most of what is in season (i.e., "What's good in May? Asparagus—and we're all the happier for it! The British season lasts just eight weeks from early May, so *make the best of it*" [*GH* May 05]).

Certain sentences stress the link between particular weather conditions, linked to the season, and food, as in "I [...] eat it for supper on those nights *when it feels almost too hot to eat*" (*GH* Jun. 05) and "There's *something reassuring* about the splutter of sausages in a pan, especially in the *chill of winter*" (*GH* Feb. 04). In other cases, the connection with the yearly rhythm involves being also attuned with the feasts and celebrations which the months bring along—above all Christmas and Easter. In these cases, the emphasis is on respecting British culinary traditions as in "The perfect *traditional* Christmas lunch" and in "Boxing Day as it should be" (in an article where turkeys and Christmas puddings are the main characters) (*GH* Dec. 04); "Fish is *traditional* on *Good Friday*"; "for *Easter Sunday* lunch it just has to be the new season's lamb"; "but *Easter* wouldn't be the same without chocolate" (*GH* Apr. 04). The above mentioned examples refer to a Western, Christian culture, which indicates a Western, Christian community of readers who are familiar with both the food restrictions (i.e., no meat allowed on Good Friday) and the food amenities of the feast (i.e., chocolate, pudding), as well as with the symbolic value played by certain dishes within their culture (i.e., the traditionally eaten lamb, symbol of Christ's sacrifice). Readers are expected to respect the traditions as underlined by the use of the semi-modal verb ("has to be"), the most common form to mark personal obligation, of the modal verb "should," which provides a hedged expression of obligation typically considered more polite, and of the modal in a negative form ("wouldn't be"), which is here used to mark prediction: there is apparently little freedom of choice for the discourse community to decide whether or not to keep the food traditions of the period. Thus, by implicitly accepting their culinary customs, *Good Housekeeping* readers confirm their cultural identity and values.

The Connection between Time and Healthy Eating

The suggestion to buy, cook and eat what is in season, following the productive cycles of nature, leads to the connection between time and a healthy way of eating. In this case, time is seen in the sense of both slow food (i.e., "like all the best things in life, artichokes require you to work a bit. It's my attempt *to fight back against the fast food movement*" (*GH* Mar. 04) and of the time needed for ingredients to be grown in a natural way (i.e., "Try to find ones [tomatoes] that have been *ripened on the vine* and have seen some sun" and "British asparagus is a treat [...] and I like the fact that it has *such a short season*—it reminds me that food comes from nature which is never a bad thing in these must-have-it-now times") (*GH* Jun. 05). This also involves the concept of organic food and home-grown products as in "Most of the fruit and veg for the cookery school and restaurant here [...] come from *our own two-acre organic garden* and *we grow everything* from tomatoes to berries and grapes" (*GH* Jun. 05). The insistence on "healthy" eating is certainly related to the editorial policy of *Good Housekeeping* that, since its first publication, has always paid great attention to the issue of good health and wholesomeness, which, for example, explains the absence of cigarette advertising on its pages.[15]

The stress on home-grown products results in suggesting readers to prefer buying their ingredients at the local shopkeepers as the following examples clearly show: "the food tends to reflect the seasons and I shop at our *local market* each Friday" or "I'll go for smoked salmon or a smoked salmon tart from the *local* deli" or "I may serve *locally made* ice cream" (*GH* Oct. 04) and

> courgettes are one of the few things I bother growing myself. They're fantastic fresh from the garden [...] For me, other summer veg comes from *local farm shops*"; "What's good in June? We love celery *fresh from a local farmers' market*"; "It's that glorious time of year when *farmers'*

---

[15] Ellen McCracken, *Decoding Women's Magazines: From* Mademoiselle *to* Ms (London, Macmillan, 1993), 181.

markets and shops are bursting with the show-off colours of nature's warm-weather bounty. (*GH* Jun. 05)

Once again, the first person narrative voice of the significant text-writer (usually a famous cook or journalist or artist) presents her/his choices as a right model to follow. Readers/food lovers are, thus, invited to eat in a salubrious way which follows the seasonal production, not only avoiding expensive firstlings, but also supporting British products as "British raspberries taste so much *better than the imported fruit* that's flown halfway around the world" (*GH* Jun. 05).

The Connection between Past Times and Eating/Cooking

This recipe was passed on to Cookery Editor Emma Marsden by her grandmother. Typed on a piece of paper, worn with age, it was titled The Royal Recipe for the Xmas Pudding Made For His Majesty The King. We believe it was made for Edward VII and, when we cooked it in the *Good Housekeeping* kitchens, the aromas filling the air were the ones Emma remembers so well from childhood. (*GH* Nov. 04)

The emphasis on eating healthily, on following the natural rhythm of food ingredients and on keeping culinary traditions, is linked with the representation of time as "time past." In quite a few cookery articles of the corpus, readers are offered traditional recipes or cooking tips inherited by mothers or family members. The above quoted paragraph, for example, connects the recipe given in today's magazine to an old dish. The details of the aged look of the recipe ("worn") with its old-fashioned title, dating to nearly a century before, stress the importance of tradition while cooking, at the same time highlighting its pleasant validity today. The "aromas" mentioned at the end introduce a sensuous element which is often linked to the smell of good food. However, the important aspect of the experience narrated is that food acts as a memory filter, carrying people back to their past, and that childhood memories are often connected with food. Food, therefore, evokes (usually) nice memories of the text-writer/cook, and is connected to the concept of family values and nearly always of one's own childhood as the following examples show:

The sweet smell of strawberries reminds me of my childhood—eating as many as I could at the pick-your-own strawberry fields and going home with a sticky red face. Strawberries were only available in summer and were a real treat. (*GH* Jun. 05)

> On crisp winter mornings, with icicles hanging off the drainpipes, Mother would make flapjacks—stirring them in a thick, pitted aluminium pan and leaving them to settle on the back of the Aga. [...] I had to be held back from eating the whole tray. (*GH* Mar. 05)

> Mother instilled me a love of food and a respect for ingredients [...].We'd often have 30 people to lunch, so whenever I wandered into the kitchen I would always be given a job. Then I'd sit, my nose barely reaching the table, and listen to the adults discuss whether or not asparagus was in season. (*GH* Mar. 05)

These examples underline how each period of the year has its own food (i.e., strawberries in summer), which accompanies the passing of time, and that people used to respect this fact (see the discussions about asparagus season).Memories of food are connoted by positive nouns (i.e., "treat," "love," "respect"), and adjectives (i.e., "sweet," "crisp"); they also see the presence of activity verbs (i.e., "to eat," "to go," "to make," "to stir," "to wander," "to sit") denoting actions and events where the person who recounts his/her food memories introduces her/himself as a busy agent. The presence of memories involves the use of a narrative mode rich in past tenses.

Not surprisingly kitchen memories are generally associated with mothers who hand down love for food, recipes and techniques to their children, as in "My mother taught me to steam fish" (*GH* Mar. 05). A few exceptions to the role of the "mother" as the family cook can be found in *GH* Dec. 04 and Mar. 05 where fathers help cooking, while texts referring to modern times see quite a few husbands and wives working together towards a meal. Humorous remarks can also be found such as "My mum taught me how not to cook. She tried her best but nothing came out right—burnt cakes and tough stews were her specialities" (*GH* Mar. 05).

Memories also enhance good traditional British ingredients which are considered worth being treasured. The following example describes a wholesome and reasoned way of eating in the past which may be seen in contrast with our modern time with its fast foods and prepared packed meals which are elsewhere judged as "garbage":

> I don't know whether my mother consciously applied intellect to our food or whether she bought what she fancied cooking, but we ate a balanced diet. I can still see the lilac Formica table, permanently heaped with fruit. [...] Most meals started with proper soup, and the main course was always accompanied by a large quantity of fresh vegetables. Even more miraculously, they were not overcooked, my mother being a big fan of Elizabeth David, Tante Marie and Constance Spry. (*GH* Feb. 04)

A good example of the link between food, tradition and individual memories is offered in the next quotation, where realistic data (i.e., "the Co-op butcher") are inserted to support the ideal, idyllic recollected atmosphere:

> The festivities would start on Christmas Eve with the dining table set with all the best cutlery and glasses [...]. Christmas morning was one of the rare occasions when my father helped with the cooking, but there was always laughter as he and my mother worked—and tippled—away together. [...] We always had turkey, too—an enormous one stuffed with the Co-op butcher's special sage and onion recipe [...]. The traditional pudding followed and leftovers were fried next morning for breakfast.[...]secretly I think Christmas isn't really Christmas without turkey, all the trimmings and plenty of spiced red cabbage. (*GH* Dec. 04)

The pages following this introductory text include all the practical information one needs for a traditional Christmas lunch and therefore link the memories of the text writer to the likely similar memories of the readers, at the same time suggesting, in a rather conservative way, that alternative menus are not advised.

The Connection between Modern Times
and Women's Cooking

> Work, family, friends, gym, chores—no wonder there never seem to be enough hours in the day! Trying to fit in all these commitments can feel like a major challenge sometimes. That's where Seeds of Change can help with its extensive range of wholesome organic products with the emphasis on taste and quality as much as convenience. So it's easy to create a delicious meal even when you don't have much time. [...] Whether you've got friends dropping by, are facing a family dinner dilemma or want to cook a cosy meal for two, there's as recipe for every occasion. (*GH* Nov. 04)

The previous representations of time are in contrast with the most recurrent image presented by the cookery articles of the corpus. The relationship between food and time in modern society, and in the lives of the discourse community of women here addressed, is not based on a relaxed, "natural" pace, but on a frantic rhythm, which sees women as cooks/eaters always fighting against their *lack* of time. Women's lack of time, caused by leading pressured lives, is the most emphasized aspect of the corpus, as every issue of the magazine has at least one of the three usual cookery articles dedicated to suggestions on how to cook with very little time available. As underlined by the promotional message quoted above, women have a load of commitments—work coming before family, social life and leisure time—which requires more time than it is available. Most of the articles of the corpus, in fact, try to balance contrasting elements such as family and social life with long work hours out of home, tasty ("delicious") with healthy ("wholesome organic") food, little time to prepare a meal with good results, stress with relax.

A look at some of the titles of the cookery articles will confirm this idea: "What busy women cook for dinner" (*GH* Jan. 04); "Quick suppers with just five ingredients" (*GH* Apr. 04); "The 30-minute supper challenge" (*GH* May 04); "20 midweek suppers—and they're all ready in 20 minutes or less!" (*GH* Sept. 04); "Busy women share their secrets of easy entertaining" (*GH* Oct. 04); "Last-minute Christmas pudding" and "Shortcuts to easy party food" (*GH* Dec. 04); "The totally stress-free way to throw a party" (*GH* Jan. 05); "What laidback cooks do for dinner parties" (*GH* Mar. 05); "15 minutes until supper's ready!" (*GH* May 05); "No planning required" (*GH* Jun. 05). These titles present contradictory adjectives referring to women seen as both (certainly) "busy" and (hopefully) "laidback," where the addressee is highly involved in her everyday activities but still capable of relaxing as far as cooking is concerned. The rapidity of the meal preparation is underlined by the modifiers ("quick"; "stress-free"; "ready"), by the metaphorical noun "shortcuts," and by the exact time details introduced ("30-minute," "last-minute," "15 minutes"). The presence of exclamative clauses underlines the relevance of the topic and its immediate appeal on the readers.

Preparing dinner is obviously a chore no woman can escape from, as underlined by the following example: "Getting the main meal of the day on the table is something women everywhere have in common, and whether you throw together leftovers at the last minute or plan ahead at the weekend, it's always great to have new ideas" (*GH* Jan. 04). In this case the concept of time is introduced by its referential elements "minute" and "weekend," the lack of time is stressed by the adjective "last" and by the action verb "to throw" with its connotation of urgency, while the concept of making good use of time is expressed by the verb "to plan" followed by the adverb "ahead," which introduces the image of a woman aspiring to be well organized and even ready to sacrifice her free time (the weekend) in order to face the kitchen chores of the week. The insistence on the term "supper" in the above quoted titles shows how this is the main meal the articles refer to. This is obviously linked to the cultural pattern of Anglo-Saxon food habits.

Being a "healthy" or a "traditional" cook is important, as we have previously noticed, but the quickness of the preparation seems to play a major role. For example, while suggesting to insert more fish in food habits, a famous cookery writer affirms that "speed" is perhaps the "most important reason "why fish is in the "premier league as far as the 21st century diet is concerned," as "it's one of the few ingredients that can provide a supper dish that's not only elegant and up-to-the-minute, but at the same time takes as little as 10 and more rarely more than 30 minutes to prepare from start to finish" (*GH* Jan. 04), where the accent on exact time data, along with the two verbs "to start" and "to finish" also associated with the notion of time, reinforces the portrait of a time conscious addressee.

The articles of the corpus consider cooking not only as a daily routine task, but as an important ritual to perform together with family and friends (as underlined by the frequent presence of the noun "party"). The social aspect of eating together is very relevant, and so there is great emphasis on easy recipes that do not need a long arrangement, but can still offer tasty, nutritious, creative dishes to be enjoyed, as underlined in the following example: "Light the fire, lay the table and prepare for a relaxed evening of luxury dining and laughter with friends—without spending hours in the kitchen" (*GH* Nov. 04). Being consistent with the already mentioned wholesome editorial policy of the magazine, the suggestion given by the articles is fundamentally to resist ready made meals which can be bought and reheated or heated up, as it is always better to prepare one's own food with basic, good ingredients, also avoiding expenses, as the following examples state:

Ready meals are an easy fall-back, but they're often laden with salt and other additives, and if you eat them often they'll send your food bill through the roof. (*GH* Feb. 04)

When life is at its most demanding, I often find myself with just half an hour to get dinner on to the table… Not always easy without resorting to pasta and a jar of sauce, but it is possible. Here are five of my favourite quick-cook recipes— and they're all far tastier than a ready meal. (*GH* May 04)

Weekday cooking can be a real chore and recent research shows that by 4 pm most of us still have no idea what we'll be cooking for dinner, that's why ready meals so often seem the most attractive option. But these speedy recipes offer a cheaper and much more nutritious solution. (*GH* Sept. 04)

When time is short, midweek cooking often has to be a speedy affair, which can make expensive, additive-laden ready meals seem an attractive option. But I always try to resist the call of the chiller cabinet...With clever shopping and these fast recipes to hand, you can rustle up simple, tasty suppers in as little time as it takes to heat up the oven and cook a shop-bought lasagne. (*GH* Feb. 05)

It is a fight of home-cooked versus mass-produced food, in a sort of anti-global attitude regarding food consumption. These examples, where a problem/solution pattern can be easily noted (Problem: "No time?", "Little time?"/Solution: "Use these recipes!"), are rich in time indicators (i.e., nouns such as "hour," references to exact timing as "4 p.m.") as well as in nouns and adjectives underlying the stressed quality of women's life today (i.e., "chore," "demanding"—this reinforced by the superlative form—, "quick[-cook]," "speedy," "short"). Even if the text-writer generally addresses her readers directly through a first person singular pronoun (i.e., "*I* often find"), her identification with the readers is total, as the use of the first person plural pronoun, an inclusive "we" (i.e., "most of us") of the second example, underlines.

The exophoric references of the introductions generally see a balance of first and second person singular pronoun or possessive adjectives, where the personal references and the direct address to the reader aim at creating the tone of an involving, friendly "conversation" between the expert and his/her public as in "I love the happy chaos involved in a big gathering. [...] *I*'ve put together a menu that fits a lively gathering of the clans [...] The big plus is that everything can be made ahead, so *you* can spend more time with *your* nearest and dearest" (*GH* Jan. 04). The Guest Cook or the Consultant Cookery Editor present themselves, then, as good models to follow in order to become a "laidback cook."

Easy dishes are, therefore, suggested and ushered in by introductory remarks such as "*Simple* cooking allows the flavour to shine through—and cuts down your *time* in the kitchen, too" (*GH* Mar. 05). The tendency is still to try to combine healthy cooking respectful of nature's rhythm with one's lack of time as the following statement affirms: "'Made with this season's fresh asparagus and the simplest of cheese sauces, this pasta dish is as quick as any supper can be,' says Moira. 'Mop up any leftover sauce with a crisp green salad'" (*GH* May 04). The informality of the language (i.e., "supper," "to mop up") adds to the friendly tone of the article, where the writer/cook proposes herself as a person with problems very similar to the reader's.

There are also "no-fuss recipes" for those who do not have much time but still want to keep up with tradition. This is the case of a "*last-minute*

Christmas pudding" or of "*Quick*-mix pastry and *shortcut* mincemeat that's whizzed together in *moments* [...] Mince pies are a prerequisite at Christmas, and this recipe is so *straightforward* you can either throw together a batch for the freezer or churn out a dozen or two *at the last minute*" (*GH* Dec. 04). This underlines the fact that, despite the hectic rhythm of our modern lives, there is the wish/will to respect traditions in the kitchen and in the dining room. Moreover, recipes which involve the use of an oven are quite recommended because they allow the possibility of doing something else while the meal is cooking, as in "I have a fondness for dishes that sit happily in the oven for an hour or so, cooking slowly while I do other things—especially on a Sunday" (*GH* Feb. 04), and in "The joy of this recipe is that it takes only five minutes of preparation, leaving you free to get on with something else while it cooks" (*GH* May 04). The oven seems to be the woman's best friend in the kitchen as it "does all the work" (*GH* Sept. 04), as many examples show, as in the following informal advice: "pop this succulent roast in the oven before your guests arrive and it looks after itself" (*GH* Nov. 04).

All the recipes give, as expected, the cooking time, but some of them underline the quickness of the preparation with a colourfully printed strip superimposed on the photo of the proposed dish, carrying minor sentences such as "SPEEDY LUNCH" (*GH* Feb. 04), "READY IN 15 MINUTES" (*GH* Jan. 05), "PREPARE IN 5 MINUTES" (*GH* Mar. 05), and "SUPER-QUICK PUD" (*GH* May 05). Also the titles of many individual recipes suggest the importance of saving time while arranging a meal, usually through the adjective "quick" as in "*Quick* Tomato Sauce" (*GH* Oct. 04), "*Quick* and easy starters," (*GH* Mar. 05), "*Quick* Camembert and Tomato Tarts" and "*Quick* Steak Supper" (*GH* Jun. 05).

The articles produce, then, the profile of a discourse community of women who are still in charge of preparing a meal, are rather short of time, supposedly because they work outside their homes, but who still enjoy cooking, more often for friends than for family, because "Yes, the food is important when you're cooking for friends, but it's really about enjoying their company" (*GH* Sept. 04) and "people are coming to see you, not judge your cooking skills" (*GH* Oct. 04). Interviews with "busy" women are often inserted where they explain how they manage to get dinner on the table or to entertain friends at the weekend despite the fact that they are "juggling work, family and the paraphernalia of everyday life" (*GH* Oct. 04). Together with their easily made recipes, they offer their own keys to success such as "never bother with more than three courses" or "don't attempt anything too ambitious" (*GH* Oct. 04). In such a way the magazine, though reinforcing the traditional role of the woman

as the being responsible for feeding the family, tries to tune to the time
constraints of contemporary society, inviting the readers to renounce
perfection and accept their limits.

From this perspective, the most common practical advice given by the
cookery articles of the corpus is to get organized as "what should be
laidback and easy can, without planning, turn into a nightmare round of
cooking, clearing and washing up" (*GH* Apr. 04). Women can be either
"prepare-ahead cooks" or "last-minute cooks" (*GH* Jan. 04). Generally
speaking *Good Housekeeping* readers are invited to organize their
cooking, to shop and prepare meals ahead of time as can be seen in the
following example, where the text-writer describes her own behaviour,
proposing it as a positive/successful model:

> I plan the recipes for the lunch, make a shopping list and draw up an action
> plan. I cook a few dishes and freeze them because it doesn't take long and
> I feel better for having made a start. I also start to stock up on a few things,
> such as the crackers, nuts and wine, to spare myself the last-minute
> pushing and shoving of an over-stuffed shopping trolley. (*GH* Dec. 04)

In one article, the Consultant Cookery Editor provides her readers with
"The stress-free time plan," where in a super-organised way readers are
told what to prepare from a month before the party takes place to an hour
before the doorbell rings and guests arrive. Suggestions on how to cheat in
style, saving time, are also given as in "No time to make a pud? Try
Waitrose Chocolate Truffle, £6.49"(*GH* Jun. 05), where the advice may be
also considered as an indirect way of advertising the product and the genre
of cookery articles mixes with the genre of promotional messages.
Sometimes explicit advice is found in shorter texts inserted within the
cookery article, framed on a side of the page, usually next to the recipe.
Either called "The get-ahead plan" or "The Key to Success," these texts
offer a collection of quick short tips, delivered through imperative clauses,
both affirmative and negative, to the readers. All the following examples
come from a few of these short texts published in the same issue:

> Prepare as much as possible in advance. I hate it when the host spends the
> whole time in the kitchen. Never bother with more than three courses,
> unless one is simply cheese. Plan the menu around the main course or a
> favourite spectacular starter.

> Make at least one course advance. Don't worry about getting the house
> perfect. Make sure none of the dishes you make requires last-minute
> synchronized cooking.

Let people cook with you and help in the kitchen. It alters the balance and eases the pressure of entertaining. Eating and talking should, above all, be sociable and fun. Far better to enjoy the conversation and let guests linger over the food than the worry too much about etiquette. Share the dinner party responsibility with friends and cook a course each.

Don't be shy about buying in food that's better than you can make yourself. The French have no qualms about this—traiteurs (part deli, part caterer) are renowned for their fabulous patés. Don't make yourself a slave in the kitchen. People are coming to see you, not judge your cooking skills.

Know your limitations. Don't attempt to cook something beyond your capabilities. Keep the meal simple. A one-pot main course is ideal. Be fully prepared, so everything is ready to go. For example, fill the kettle and have the coffee pot ready and cups on a tray. However good a cook you are, do as much ahead as you can. (*GH* Oct. 04)

These pieces of advice reveal that no one should renounce the pleasure of eating in good company, the cook has the same right as the guests to join the social gathering, having fun while providing good food. The cook has to accept her own limits both as a housewife and as a cook, she can also take advantage of food sold in shops (and the example of what French people do is not casually inserted here, as the image of gourmands and good chefs is traditionally associated with French cuisine). The social value of cooking is stressed by advice such as "let people cook with you and help in the kitchen" and "share the dinner party responsibility with friends and cook a course each." The insistence on verbs such as "to prepare," "to plan," "to make sure" underlines how organizing one's time has become a precious virtue of the ideal reader—the woman cook of today.

Getting organised means making the most of the time available, saving precious moments for other things such as enjoying family (i.e., "The big plus is that everything can be made ahead, so you can spend more time with *your nearest and dearest*" (*GH* Jan. 04), carrying on with other chores (i.e., "This roast lamb dish […] may take a while to cook, but it takes very little time to prepare and once it's in the oven, you can more or less forget about it and get on with your other *household tasks*" [*GH* Jan. 04]), or simply relaxing (i.e., "Then you'll have plenty of time *to enjoy the break* [Easter weekend] instead of spending the whole time in the kitchen" [*GH* Apr. 04]). Thus, in getting organized, women transform time from a tyrant or an enemy to fight into a precious ally.

Conclusion

The analysis of the 54 *Good Housekeeping* cookery articles present in the corpus shows various representations of time. Given the editorial policy of the magazine, which stresses the wholesomeness issue, in buying ingredients, cooking and eating them readers are invited to respect the natural cycle of nature, without forcing its time, but always respecting it. This idea leads to the concept of "slow food" in contrast with fast food, where "time" is again respected in its regular rhythm. The connection between food (generally traditionally British) and time past is another aspect present in the articles, through the culinary memories of the text-writers (often celebrities in the field of cuisine). Here the importance of keeping traditions and of passing them on to future generations is emphasized and seen as a relevant factor for the cultural identity of the discourse community of women addressed. The most recurrent aspect of time in the corpus is, however, based on the connection between modern times and eating/cooking. Though insisting on the traditional profile of a woman seen within a family context and in charge of feeding her beloved ones, these articles show how women run against time, trying to fulfil their many commitments of today. The continuous lack of time imposes new rules to women, who have to learn how to be perfectly organized, often renouncing their ideals of perfection. Ready-made meals are discouraged, in favour of simple, quick meals prepared by the hostess. The stress is on the social aspect of eating together, an aspect nobody should renounce to, which may involve sharing the preparation of the meals with friends. These articles reinforce the idea that "food is a vehicle for expressing friendship—or at least acceptance, for smoothing social intercourse, for showing concern."[16] In sum, the cookery articles provide an interesting profile of their ideal reader, a woman who has a role in society as a working person who earns her living, is free to organise her daily life, is tuned to the time constraints of contemporary society, fights her own battle against globalization in food consumption within her own domestic sphere, still defending her values based on the importance of family and social life. The articles also suggest to consider cooking a pleasure and an important aspect of everyday life, more than a domestic burden to carry, as perfectly expressed by this final example from the corpus which affirms that

---

[16] Paul Fieldhouse, *Food and Nutrition: Customs and Culture* (London, Croom Helm, 1986), 75.

Cooking can be life-enhancing. There's pleasure to be had from working with fresh ingredients and releasing their most enticing flavours. How miserable, then, when cooking becomes a tyranny—a day-in, day-out obligation to put a meal on the table. For me, the ideal is a balance between real cooking and convenience food as a back-up for days when work or play has sapped my energy. There's nothing wrong with beans on toast every now and then. These reliable recipes are the ones I reach for when I feel like eating something familiar—dishes that warm the heart and soul. (*GH* Nov. 04)

Bibliography

Benn's Media. *The Guide to United Kingdom Newspapers, Periodicals, Television, Radio and On-line Media.* Vol. 1: United Kingdom (2003).

Bhatia, Vijay K. *Worlds of Written Discourse.* New York: Continuum, 2004.

Biber, Douglas, Susan Conrad and Randi Reppen. *Corpus Linguistics: Investigating Language Structure and Use.* Cambridge: Cambridge University Press, 2002.

Chiavetta, Eleonora. "A Passion for British Food: A Discourse Analysis of Cookery Articles in Magazines." *Interactions* (Spring 2004): 31-43.

Fairclough, Norman. *Discourse and Social Change.* Cambridge: Polity Press, 1992.

—. *Critical Discourse Analysis.* Harlow: Longman, 1995.

—. *Language and Power.* Harlow: Longman, 2001.

Fieldhouse, Paul. *Food and Nutrition: Customs and Culture.* London: Croom Helm, 1986.

Görlach, Manfred. "Text-types and Language History: The Cookery Recipe." In *History of Englishes: New Methods and Interpretations in Historical Linguistics.* Ed. Matti Rissanen, Ossi Ihalainen, Terttu Nevalainen, and Irma Taavitsainen. Berlin: Mouton de Gruyter, 1992. 736-61.

Hennessy, Brendan. *Writing Feature Articles: A Practical Guide to Methods and Markets.* Oxford: Heinemann, 1989.

McCracken, Ellen. *Decoding Women's Magazines. From* Mademoiselle *to* Ms. London: Macmillan, 1993.

Montanari, Massimo. *Il cibo come cultura.* Roma: Editori Laterza, 2004.

Stubbs, Michael. *Text and Corpus Analysis.* Oxford: Blackwell, 1996.

Swales, John M. *Genre Analysis.* Cambridge: Cambridge University Press, 1990.

CHAPTER NINE

WRITING WOMEN, WRITING FOOD: AFRICAN-AMERICAN WOMEN'S COOKBOOKS IN HISTORICAL PERSPECTIVE

HÉLÈNE LE DANTEC-LOWRY

Introduction: Cookbooks as Historical Sources

The inclusion of the study of women into American historiography, which grew after the 1960s, has profoundly altered the writing of history in the United States. Some of the most innovative publications in the field of late have examined the correlation between women and food, adding much to our understanding of the place and role of women in the American society.[1] Historians of women and gender have investigated sources that had largely been ignored until the 1960s, finally giving a voice to women by analyzing letters, memoirs, biographies, and diaries. Recipe books—written by hand and passed down from mother to daughter throughout the

---

[1] Among the books published on this subject is the pioneer study by Laura Shapiro, *Perfection Salad: Women and Cooking at the Turn of the Century* (New York: The Modern Library, 2001[1986]), followed by other interesting works such as *Cooking Lessons: The Politics of Gender and Food*, ed. Sherrie A. Inness (New York: Rowman & Littlefield, 2001); Mary Drake McFreely, *Can She Bake a Cherry Pie? American Women and the Kitchen in the Twentieth Century* (Amherst: University of Massachusetts Press, 2001); Janet Theophano, *Eat My Words: Reading Women's Lives Through the Cookbooks They Wrote* (New York: Palgrave, 2002); Jessamyn Neuhaus, *Manly Meals and Mom's Home Cooking: Cookbooks and Gender in Modern America* (Baltimore: Johns Hopkins University Press, 2003); Laura Schenone, *A Thousand Years Over a Hot Stove: A History of Women Told Through Food, Recipes, and Remembrances* (New York: W. W. Norton & Co., 2003); and Laura Shapiro, *Something From the Oven: Reinventing Dinner in 1950s America* (New York: Viking, 2004).

eighteenth and nineteenth centuries—along with cookbooks published by female writers, are now included in the writings used by historians, and attest to the intimate connection between women and the kitchen. Cookbooks can be seen as historical documents, which "reveal much about the societies that produce them" and show how "foods, food preparation, kitchen labor, gender, class, and race have intersected in the United States."[2] Published cookbooks as historical sources may not tell us everything, and it is difficult to know how they were used by the women who bought them: which recipes they chose to prepare, which ones they rejected, whether any were altered. It is also hard to know whether the women who bought these books actually cooked from them, used them regularly, or passed them on. Only sociological studies would provide information on these points, but I am not aware of any extensive works as yet published. Still, cookbooks can tell us much about their authors, the community or class they come from, or the readership they intend to reach.

Cookbooks are also useful for their representation of food and of the women who write them. For a long time, cookbooks emanated from white middle-class women who initially saw them as manuals to inform others from their own group about proper conduct for preparing food and serving it. They helped keep a class structure together while also reflecting the discourse on women's place, on the family, and on nutrition at a given time in history. Through these works, women reformers at the end of the nineteenth century, for example, also intended to change the ways the poor ate, thinking that food was a clear moral and social indicator of class, or they sought to influence the food habits of recent immigrants, in an attempt to Americanize them to what was considered the American diet, largely based on bland and homogeneous recipes from New England. Even books published about the food of immigrants often transformed the original recipes in an effort to render them palatable to a mostly white middle-class readership. Still, other voices were sometimes heard. African-American women, the main focus of the research presented here, were involved in cookbook-writing starting at the end of the Civil War and after the abolition of slavery. What is thought to be the first such book by a black woman can be found at the Schlesinger Library at Harvard University; it dates back to 1881 and was "spoken" by an illiterate black woman.[3] However, cookbooks as such were rare and most works by black

---

[2] Neuhaus, 1.

[3] I thank Nancy Cott, faculty director of the Schlesinger Library, for bringing this to my attention. The book in question is *What Mrs. Fisher Knows about Old Southern Cooking* by Abby Fisher. In an appendix to *Black Hunger. Soul Food*

women are quite recent. Moreover, those written by African-American women were mostly published by small companies or by the authors themselves, and were not widely circulated. It is in great part due to the impact of the civil rights movement and the increased inclusion of black authors and culture into mainstream literature that cookbooks by African-American women became more common.[4] I propose to examine a few of these works and to show how they comprise part of an American genre of cookbook writing, while at the same time showing their own specificities due to the unique history and culture of African-Americans in the United States.

African-American Women and Food: An Intimate Connection

I will focus on recent publications for several reasons. The "recipe books" written by hand in the eighteenth and nineteenth centuries were almost exclusively produced by white women. By contrast black women were rarely literate. Their tradition was based exclusively on orality, and recipes would have thus been transmitted by voice and through visual example, and committed to the memory of the recipient that way (to a daughter or another close kin, a friend, or a member of the same church, for instance).

It must be pointed out as well that throughout American history, black women have often been associated with cooking and represented as cooks, to the point of caricature,[5] as attested by their presence as cinematographic icons, literary characters or advertising figures. In the American culture of representation, the black woman was more often than not portrayed as the faithful mammy of slavery, the spirited domestic, or the Aunt Jemima on boxes of pancake mix. This is not necessarily true any longer, but those

---

and America (Minneapolis: University of Minnesota Press, 2004[1999]), Doris Witt has compiled a very useful bibliography of cookbooks by African-American authors.

[4] Rafia Zafar, "The Signifying Dish: Autobiography and History in Two Black Women's Cookbooks," in *Food in the USA: A Reader*, ed. Carole M. Counihan (New York: Routledge, 2002), 249-62.

[5] Stereotypical representations of the black servant—cooks included—can be seen in the following works, among others: Deborah Gray White, *A'rn't I a Woman? Female Slaves in the Plantation South* (New York: W. W. Norton, 1985); and Stephanie Cole, "A White Woman, of Middle Age Would Be Preferred: Children's Nurses in the Old South," in *Neither Lady nor Slave: Working Women of the Old South*, ed. Susanna Delfino and Michelle Gillespie (Chapel Hill: The University of North Carolina Press, 2002), 75-101.

images are never very far from the collective American psyche. Paradoxically though, and in spite of the persistent mammy stereotype, black women's contribution to southern cooking and to American cuisine in general was often ignored, and the emancipation of slaves did not alter this situation. As white women in the South were trying to reconstruct a specifically southern identity after the Civil War and the abolition of slavery, they insisted on aspects of southern culture that connected them to a certain past. They did not reject the "cult of domesticity" prevailing in the rest of the country at the time, but instead tried to make it their own. This was done in at least two ways: by producing images and representations of the black mammy and cook as models of subservience and attachment to the family of their white owners, and by co-opting some of the Blacks' contributions to southern culture. Thus, the faithful servants could not be shown as what they really were: slaves whose lives and deaths were controlled by the dominant white class. Similarly, southern white women would correspond to feminine ideals at the time through their writing of recipe collections; indeed they fulfilled a requirement of Victorian homemakers by showing their will and pleasure in feeding their family. Some white women, mostly of the ruling classes, published cookbooks about the cuisine of the South, but they rarely acknowledged that a majority of the recipes had been created, elaborated, prepared by their (often enslaved) black cooks. African-American women were erased from southern culinary culture by writers who were trying to recover the lost identity of the former plantation mistress; the contributions of slaves could not be included in such a pattern. Many black women have found it hard to face such stereotypical visions, which affirm "that Blacks 'naturally' wish to serve whites," even at the expense of their identity as slaves and as members of an oppressed community.[6] As a consequence, some have turned away from the kitchen and have refused to be associated with cooking or cookbooks.[7]

At the same time, it cannot be denied that, for decades, black women experienced food—cooking, selling and finding it—as a way to survive or to resist exploitation and oppression. The link between African-American women and culinary history is, therefore, logical in many ways and cannot be easily ignored when one looks at American history. Before emancipation, the slave cooks sometimes enjoyed privileges the majority

---

[6] Sherrie Inness, *Secret Ingredients: Race, Gender, and Class at the Dinner Table* (New York: Palgrave Macmillan, 2006), 106.
[7] For various reasons, their refusal converged with that of the feminists of the 1970s who backed out of kitchen duties and turned away from representations associated with the exploitation and subservient place of women in the society.

of other enslaved Blacks did not. For example, they could use their skills as leverage when dealing with masters who could not always easily replace them, or they were sometimes allowed to raise money by selling part of the food they made in order to buy freedom for themselves or their relatives, as testified in Harriet Jacobs's famous autobiography. Free women, and some slaves, could also sell food (produce or meat, but also prepared dishes) in city markets. This trend increased during the period of Reconstruction (1865-1877) when former slaves could move about more freely and when many decided to migrate to cities—southern urban centers at first—for better work opportunities. Over 90% of black women became domestics, and food preparation was one of their favored occupations: being a cook was a coveted position, brought better pay, allowed them more flexible hours than other servants, and also provided opportunities to secure extra food for themselves and their families. Whenever they could, urbanized Blacks also tended their own vegetable patch and, again, some started small businesses by managing lunch carts and catering services.[8] One of the ways black women provided for themselves and their family when they migrated North after slavery was by managing food stalls, starting small restaurants or catering businesses, or working as cooks. As discrimination and segregation kept African-Americans in an inferior economic position, procuring food was one of the major worries for a black woman. Food has been at the heart of black survival, and cookbooks published by African-American women testify to this history. Concurrently, as has been true for American women in general, cooking has always involved domestic labor with much repetition and drudgery, but it also incorporates pleasure and creativity that often leads to recognition and admiration by relatives, friends and one's community. Food has also been associated with rejoicing and celebration when used in family and community feasts and rituals. It is thus not surprising that black women have also decided to write their own cookbooks.

African-American Women's Cookbooks as Inscribed in an American Culinary Tradition

Most cookbooks by African-American women are not simply collections of recipes with specific ingredients and the precise procedure on how to

---

[8] Tera W. Hunter, *To 'Joy My Freedom: Southern Black Women's Lives and Labors after the Civil War* (Cambridge: Harvard University Press, 1997), especially chapter 3.

prepare a dish; they are also interwoven with recollections and memories associated with the writer's life, her family and the African-American community in general. The examples I have chosen to examine fall in that category. In that regard, these works are not very different from a common American genre of cookbook-writing, in which personal reminiscences and story-telling are widely used. They become "the stage on which [women] unfold a personal, family, and cultural drama."[9] This reenactment of familial and group experiences is found in a diversity of African-American cookbooks. An example can be found in the community and association cookbooks so familiar to American readers. In *The Black Family Reunion Cookbook*,[10] many recipes are identified by the name of their creator, but are also set next to a short text in which a specific person, identified by name and place of residence, recounts a memory about the described dish. Such memories often reach back to childhood or even to previous generations, creating a link with a community, a region, or a family, and making the book a communal effort that tends to transcend geographical and class differences. These cookbooks help preserve tradition and they construct or maintain community. Similarly, in *Soul Food* Sheila Ferguson describes this type of cooking as "a legacy clearly steeped in tradition [...] handed down from generation to generation, from one black family to another,"[11] further enhancing a common narrative shared by all Blacks in the United States and preserved over time. The popular book by the Darden sisters, *Spoonbread and Strawberry Wine: Recipes and Reminiscences of a Family,* tells of family memories, as clearly stated in its title, and includes photographs and family portraits along with the recipes collected by the writers on a journey through the South, whence their family originated, and during which they traced back kin ancestry and cultural roots. This book is seen by its authors as a "pilgrimage 'home,' which revealed to us not only good food but the origins, early struggles, and life-styles of our family."[12] Another example is Maya Angelou's recent book,[13] in which the famous writer introduces

---

[9] Theophano, 1.

[10] *The Black Family Reunion Cookbook: Recipes and Food Memories*, From the National Council of Negro Women (New York: Fireside-Simon & Schuster, 1993).

[11] Sheila Ferguson, *Soul Food: Classic Cuisine from the Deep South* (New York: Grove Press, 1989), viii.

[12] Norma Jean and Carole Darden, *Spoonbread and Strawberry Wine: Recipes and Reminiscences of a Family* (New York: Doubleday, 1994[1978]), xiv-xv.

[13] Maya Angelou, *Hallelujah! The Welcome Table: A Lifetime of Memories with Recipes* (London: Virago Press, 2005).

each recipe with a long description of the circumstances in which a particular dish was made, served and eaten. Her book also encapsulates lifelong memories, functioning, it seems, as a testimony of her accomplishments and adventures and as a witness of her encounters with a variety of people and experiences.

Books by African-American women use the same pattern as many works by other women in the United States: they have a biographical function and some are clearly autobiographical; they preserve history—of individual, family and community—and sometimes re-create it as the author fictionalizes her own story, changing it at times to make it more poignant, glamorous or difficult. The book and its recipes also become a chronicle and a representation of a specific character by re-placing her in a given context. The author makes specific choices concerning the recipes she opts to include, but also about the material around them; these can be short descriptions of persons associated with a recipe, an ingredient, or a place, but they can also be drawings, maps or photographs. All these encapsulate the gastronomic experience of the writer, but also, at times, of her family or community in a specific social class, ethnic group or region. Beyond being informative about a particular cuisine and providing recipes the reader can reproduce, these books clearly function as collage works, with both symbolic and suggestive effects. They are similar in this way to photo albums, personal diaries or travel logs and enable their writers to affirm themselves through a personal voice, using the pronoun "I," representative of a specific individual but also, more generally of a woman's voice. Vertamae Smart-Grosvernor's books, such as *Vibration Cooking: Or the Travel Notes of a Geechee Girl* (1970), fit this description, even if they cannot be reduced to this function only, as do the books by the Darden sisters and Maya Angelou, even though they were published at different times. These works tell of specific events and places that are part of a larger culinary adventure. Over time, and up to the present, many cookbooks by American women, whether by colonial settlers, farm women in the west, or immigrants, among others, have been consistent with this descriptive and memorial concept. Black women were not among the early contributors to this genre, for the reasons evoked earlier (poverty and illiteracy, segregation and racism, refusal of stereotyping), but they are now increasingly part of American gastronomic literature. Even if cookbooks can be seen as symbols of the confinement of women to the kitchen, they also hint at the desire of female writers to become emancipated through their work, which they describe and reproduce through chosen recipes, making it at last visible and recognizable. Black writers follow the same logic.

Cookbooks Written by African-American Women as Unique Endeavors

Despite their common traits, it would be erroneous to see African-American cookbooks as no different from those written by other women in the United States. Due to the specificities of the history of Blacks in the U.S. and their place in society, they have a specific role. Women's cookbooks in general are helpful to reclaim a history that has often been neglected, ignored or put aside as less relevant to the evolution of the United States. They offer traces and signs that women participated in nation building through their work in the kitchen, a place often correctly associated with imprisonment and limitations on female development, but one that should also be considered in terms of creativity and agency. This can of course be said of some of the cookbooks written by immigrant women and by members of minority groups in general, but it is particularly important for black women since culinary activities provided opportunities they could find in few other places throughout much of their history. As has sometimes been the case in the writing of women's history in general, there has been a debate over whether spaces restricted for women were places of oppression that needed to be destroyed, transformed or shared with men to erase their female-only specificities, or whether these spaces (the kitchen being a primary one along with the home or the family) could actually be considered as sites of female power and decision making. It seems fruitless to argue in favor of one aspect as both seem relevant to me. The kitchen was indeed a symbol of Black oppression and exploitation in the context of a white-owned home in which the black women worked as domestics, but it was also one of the few places that afforded these women some form of recognition for their talent, creativity, and inventiveness as cooks. It would also be wrong to forget that black women cooked in their own kitchen as well, however small and poorly equipped they may have been by white middle-class standards. These were indeed places of repetitive, hard work—as it was for all women—and were further cause for frustration when poverty meant women had to do with very little to feed their own kin. Still, they were also rooms where black women derived satisfaction from cooking for their family and from creating dishes for Sunday dinners, church events, feasts and celebrations that established them as recognized pillars of their family and community. Today still, cooking and selling homemade foods are very much part of fundraising events in the Black community, whether it be for a church, a school program, or for poorer members of the community. These actions give women an important place within their kin and peer groups. This applies to many American women, but the racism and oppression against African-Americans and their resilience as human beings and as members of the black community have given a particularly prominent role to the black cook. Black cookbook writers have taken this into account, and their works have consequently adopted specific attributes and qualities.

Writing up the recipes of their past and of their communities has enabled these women to identify a certain cuisine as their own; this is particularly true for southern cuisine, because black women were often excluded from the "story telling" about the South. By giving their own version of fried chicken, gumbos, pecan or sweet potato pies, and other southern classics, these women reclaim the cuisine of their ancestors and give it its rightful place in the culinary narrative of the region. By insisting on the contribution of black women to the history of their community, the South, and the U.S. in general, they pay homage to work that had been largely ignored or denigrated. By creating an uninterrupted line of cooks, from their own recipes to those of the past, they create a culinary tradition that extends beyond the white-owned kitchen and encompasses the whole Black community, solidifying "ties with other blacks, including women" and passing down "cultural lessons that might otherwise be forgotten."[14] Black writers, however, largely dissociate themselves from the stereotypes about the "mammy" or the "slave cook."[15] They are not ignoring the black domestics of the past, but try instead to include them in the culinary history of the Black community and of the nation as a whole as characters who were not merely defined by their work for the Whites. The recipe books written by African-American women rectify some of the wrong done to Blacks in general and to black women in particular. By reading them and using them we no longer ignore the fact that African-American cuisine has a continuing and vibrant history in the United States.

Poverty is one of the main stereotypes associated with African-Americans. Even though a black bourgeoisie emerged during Reconstruction and grew in some of the urban ghettos after the migration to northern industrial centers, the common image of blacks, women included, has often been of people mired in poor neighborhoods with the associated ills of malnourishment, inadequate housing, broken families, violence and crime. This is a persistent image today, in spite of the growth of a black middle class.

Some African-American cookbook authors sometimes emphasize their ties to a black bourgeoisie in an effort to escape association with

---

[14] Inness, *Secret*, 113.

[15] See Theopano; Cole; and Inness, *Secret*.

stereotypical black poverty. This is true of the Darden sisters, whose book contains many references to the middle-class professions held by their forefathers and to the prominent roles these people played in their communities. The authors remind us, for example, that a local high school in Wilson, North Carolina was named after their grandfather, who was head of the trustee board of his church,[16] and that their mother was a devoted community worker.[17] By focusing on the bourgeois lifestyle of their forebears, the Dardens show clearly that poverty was not the only reality of the black group, and that its bourgeoisie should be acknowledged for its sophisticated—and somewhat idealized—cooking and living habits. The examples they give of dinner parties and the photographs of well-dressed people and large houses attest to this. The inclusion of many recipes for beauty creams and lotions is not only a way to remember and preserve these old-fashioned preparations used by women for skincare; they may also be a means to indicate and stress that black women of the more affluent class paid much attention to their looks, and that beauty is also one of the defining elements of Black culture. Their work can be considered as an "autoethnographic cookbook, a form which seeks both to represent the group within its own sense of its history and culture and to contradict dominant representations."[18]

Rafia Zafar remarks that the Darden sisters were from the northern bourgeoisie and had been raised in a manner that was very different from that of some of their relatives in the South. They were perhaps trying to bridge "the ever-widening gap between the Black working class and the bourgeoisie"[19] at a time (their book was first published in 1978) when a growing middle class was seizing the new opportunities offered by the desegregationist and anti-discriminatory laws passed in the 1960s. It is interesting to note as well that the family life that emerges from their book—a well-knit and sharing network of extended kin—ran counter to the prevailing view of the black family as dysfunctional and problem-ridden, which had been popularized by the Moynihan report of 1965 and its various media interpretations. The common mention of men as participants in cooking for their family and their portrayal, to a certain extent, as stable providers and almost patriarchal figures may also have

---

[16] Darden and Darden, 5-6.
[17] Darden and Darden, 214.
[18] Arlene Voski Avakian and Barbara Haber, "Feminist Food Studies: A Brief History," in *From Betty Crocker to Feminist Food Studies: Critical Perspectives on Women and Food*, ed. Arlene Voski Avakian and Barbara Haber (Amherst: University of Massachusetts Press, 2005), 19.
[19] Zafar, 256.

helped the authors denounce the popular myth of the emasculating Black matriarch that many derived from Moynihan's report. The families portrayed by the Dardens parallel the more normative model emphasized by the dominant white society. The role of women is not diminished by these and other cookbook writers, however, and there are many examples of strong, focused and organized black women who participate actively in the economy of their family and know how to take a stand for their relatives, as is shown for instance by Maya Angelou when she recalls how her grandmother slapped a teacher who had dared lay her hands on her mute granddaughter because she had supposedly refused to speak in class.[20]

Many female writers actually provide recipes by male relatives and friends, demonstrating how food also served as an economic outlet for black men, who became cooks, caterers and restaurant managers. Men also sometimes chose food-related jobs and took risks as self-employed food workers because other more traditional male jobs were simply not available to them due to racist and segregationist practices. At least until quite recently, the tradition of cookbooks by and for Whites made a clearer distinction between male and female cooks, women being shown as the everyday, almost fastidious, cook, keeping the family fed and happy, while men were depicted as more natural chefs, preparing an elaborate cuisine or tending a barbecue.[21] This distinction is much less evident in cookbooks by black women, which occasionally describe everyday cooking by men. Throughout American history, cooking was not only a way to survive economically for many Blacks, for both men and women, it also provided a path to creativity and recognition that they could not obtain otherwise in a segregated and racist nation. African-American female writers recognize this past by including recipes, cooking tricks and advice provided by the men of their family or entourage. By doing so, they also pay homage to the men around them and give them a place in their family and community that the white-dominated society would often refuse to grant them. The mention of recipes by white men in Angelou's book also shows an evolving society in which interracial relations are becoming more acceptable, at least for this famous black writer.

The Dardens' cookbook offers a view of the black community that stresses the existence of economic and social diversity. Maya Angelou's book and also Smart-Grosvernor's, refer to the plurality of African-American experience: both mention instances of personal poverty along

---

[20] Angelou, 17.
[21] Neuhaus; Shapiro, *Something*.

with recollections that clearly set them in a higher class bracket. In some ways, Angelou's book conveys the notion of a "legitimate" black middle class. Even though she describes how she was raised in poverty, she then goes on to refer to her travels, her encounters with famous people, and her meals in restaurants in various cities, indicating that she has now left poverty behind. This seems to point out that black cooking and, by extension, the African-American community, cannot be associated just with poverty only.

Black women writers are also careful to show the diversity of black culinary heritage, acknowledging the contribution of people from various geographical, social and cultural origins, while avoiding an overly-stated reference to the former slave South. Such was the case when Freda De Knight, the editor of the well-known African-American magazine *Ebony*, published a collection of recipes that came from various places across the United States and the black Diaspora.[22] This is also true of a more recent work by Diane Spivey, who includes chapters on the foods of Africa and Latin America as well as the United States, the South included. She inscribes black American cooking in a world perspective that includes various communities dispersed through the slave trade, presenting them into a diasporic community with common roots, the African continent being acknowledged as the original birthplace from which ingredients and methods dispersed. Spivey set out "to grasp and document the unique transition and contribution of African cooking to cuisines throughout the world [...]" and claims to "have been on a Mission."[23] The fiction writer Ntozake Shange said in the introduction to her own cookbook *If I Can Cook/You Know God Can*, that she set out to mix "history, literature, vernacular, culture, and philosophy, 'long with absolutely fabulous receipts [...] meant to open our hearts and minds to what it means for black folks in the western hemisphere to be full," [24] thus including other black groups in the Americas.

Maya Angelou starts her book with memories of her childhood and of her grandmother's cooking in a poor black southern community, showing its "wealth" and superb taste despite poverty, and recognizing her grandmother and all black mothers as creative performers in the kitchen,

---

[22] Freda De Knight, *A Date with a Dish: A Cookbook of American Negro Recipes* (New York: Hermitage Press, 1948).

[23] Diane M. Spivey, *The Peppers, Cracklings, and Knots of Wool Cookbook: The Global Migration of African Cuisine* (Albany: State University of New York Press, 1999), 1.

[24] Ntozake Shange, *If I Can Cook/You Know God Can* (Boston: Beacon Press, 1998), 3.

even when they were mostly scorned outside of their group. Angelou then relates food and cooking experiences that take her out of the South into places as diverse as California (Berkeley), France and Italy, including dishes from various other cuisines around the world. She also mentions her associations with such prominent food writers as Craig Clayborne and M. F. K. Fisher. Through the experiences of this major black writer, African-American cuisine thus acquires a universal dimension that takes it away from the confines and the normative definition of the former slave states and beyond simply referring to African origins. The cultural boundaries of the American South are not necessarily shunned or ignored. Rather, they are expanded to include a much broader variety of cultures and influences from the rest of the United States, encompassing regions of the world as a whole. "Cultural syncretism" is favored over "cultural isolation"[25] and black food is no longer limited to the former slave South. To accomplish this, some writers choose to focus on the contributions of American Blacks everywhere in the United States, others emphasize the African origins within the Diaspora, and others still highlight a more "cosmopolitan" set of people and places. Through such works, black women become "active participants in the creation of a black Atlantic culture."[26] African-American food and cooking can thus be incorporated into Paul Gilroy's thesis of a Black Atlantic established through transatlantic cross-cultural exchange. When cooking or sharing their food in Europe or Africa, Angelou and Smart-Grosvenor attest to the multi-dimensional directions of this exchange and position Black cuisine in a pattern of "call and response" between black and white communities, and not just as a limited rendering of poverty and exploitation fixed within the culinary boundaries imposed by the dominant white societies.[27] In this way, black food is not reduced to innards and often despised greens—notably collard greens—so long associated with slavery, when Blacks were left with ingredients that Whites refused to eat, or with urban

---

[25] This is an argument made by Doris Witt when she examines in particular Smart-Grosvenor's cookbooks in "'My Kitchen Was the World': Vertamae Smart Grosvenor's Geechee Diaspora," in *Kitchen Culture in America: Popular Representations of Food, Gender and Race,* ed. Sherrie Inness (Philadelphia: University of Pennsylvania Press, 2001), 227-49.

[26] Doris Witt, *Black Hunger*, 176.

[27] Paul Gilroy, *The Black Atlantic: Modernity and Double Consciousness* (Cambridge: Harvard University Press, 1993). See also Doris Witt, *Black Hunger*, for the connection between Gilroy's vision and some of the conclusions that can be derived from certain African-American cookbooks, especially pages 156 and 175-80.

poverty, when lack of money made it difficult for African-Americans to buy anything but the cheapest foodstuffs. It is interesting to note that some of the ingredients and recipes understood by many Americans to define "soul food" are not commonly mentioned by black cookbook writers.[28] This may reflect their refusal to be associated with slavery and economic hardships, but probably also has much to do with the interests of the readership they were targeting. These authors were aware that many of their readers do not belong to their own racial group, and that some (perhaps even a majority) are white middle-class women who would certainly not be interested in cooking recipes that are so distant from their own culinary background and might even repulse them.

Black cookbook writers create a lineage going back to the women who cooked before them—including slave cooks and black domestics—ensuring that their contributions are integrated at last into culinary history and, more generally, into the historical narrative of the United States. At the same time, they not only reclaim the history of their people, they also re-create it to include the cuisine of Blacks everywhere, showing that African-American culinary experience cannot be limited to the time of slavery, to poverty, or to the American South, as was often believed by Whites.

By occasionally including recipes from different women, not all of them African-American, black authors create a sisterhood that extends beyond racial and class lines, illuminating the bonds that link women as cooks. Gender definition throughout American history often restricted women to the tasks of homemakers, and African-American women were commonly regarded as nothing more than hired cooks and were thus overlooked in many cookbooks. In their own writings, some black women show how this narrow vision can be reinterpreted by giving a voice to the black cook and by taking her out of the confines of a specific racial group and social class. This is particularly clear in Angelou's culinary reminiscences, in which she cites recipes given by white women friends. Of course, Angelou and Shange are both recognized writers whose position in the literary world gives them ample opportunities to associate with a wide diversity of people, including some outside of their community and even their own country. These authors may also indicate

---

[28] This is not the case for Smart-Grosvenor, who actually provides recipes for "chitterlings" and other such ingredients, and who makes regular references to her cooking them in various places, not only in the United States. Still, as Doris Witt notes in *Black Hunger*, Smart-Grosvenor has an ambiguous position as she "distanced herself from the term 'soul' while proselytizing for many of the foods associated with it" (156).

their openness, their willingness to accept others, stressing the fact that the reverse was often not true—white women rarely cited recipes by Blacks in their cookbooks. They redefine black female identity and indicate that if African-American women were cast in restricted roles and positions, including in their cooking, the same was true for white women, whose choices as cooks were also limited by rules imposed by society. Definitions of whiteness and blackness thus necessarily include factors incorporating gender and class.

Conclusion

As a whole, black women's books are far more than simple collections of recipes: they borrow from various genres and sources to create unique testimonies to the resilience and creativity of Blacks and their culture. While food acts as a "milieu of memory," these books function as "sites of memory"—to use Pierre Nora's expressions—in that their authors show a commemorative consciousness by systematically preserving the history of black cooking and of the women who performed it in the face of neglect and omission by the dominant white society.[29] These cookbooks are a repository of Black history and culture, and show that these attributes are not static and fixed in time, but instead evolve constantly and are very much alive. The authors describe what are considered as "traditional" black food and southern recipes, helping to keep them alive and on the table at a time when more Americans, including Blacks, take less time for sit-down and home-prepared family meals. They also re-interpret what black cooking is by occasionally incorporating recipes, ingredients and spices from other places and cultures, proving the versatility and creativity of black cuisine which, to them, is not just a hold-over from a bygone era that needs to be recreated. In their book, the Dardens attempted to preserve southern culture in a period, the late 1970s, when it was disappearing from their own northern lifestyle, while books by Spivey, Angelou, Smart-Grosvenor and Shange add to this culture, widening it and keeping it alive and well.

While notions of American cooking and of Americanness in general were long imposed on Blacks, in writing their own cookbooks, black women are able to show how they appropriate, accept or refuse such images and norms, providing self-definition and a sense of belonging.

---

[29] Pierre Nora's theory about memory can be found, for example, in "Between Memory and History: *Les Lieux de Mémoire*," in *History and Memory in African-American Culture*, ed. Geneviève Fabre and Robert O'Meally (New York: Oxford University Press, 1994), 284-300.

Women's voices were often invisible and cookbooks provide them—among other things—with a way to tell, to narrate their own stories, their own history. This is even more crucial for black women, whose voices were often silenced. They offer a wider definition of American cuisine, one that includes the recipes and preparations of groups other than just the white middle class. Furthermore, black female writers affirm their belonging to one community, one nation, and, by extension at times, one disaporic entity, thus also redefining what it means to be black in America.

These cookbooks by African-American women confirm the importance of these works as historical sources that offer important insight into the relations between race, gender and class in U.S. society. They show us how the authors are in a dialectical relationship between finding a place in a popular—and sometimes quite lucrative—published genre and writing political and ideological commentary on the place of black women in American history and society.

Bibliography

Angelou, Maya. *Hallelujah! The Welcome Table: A Lifetime of Memories with Recipes*. London: Virago Press, 2005.

Avakian, Arlene Voski and Barbara Haber. "Feminist Food Studies: A Brief History." In *From Betty Crocker to Feminist Food Studies: Critical Perspectives on Women and Food*. Ed. Arlene Voski Avakian and Barbara Haber. Amherst: University of Massachusetts Press. 2005. 1-26.

Cole, Stephanie. "A White Woman, of Middle Age Would Be Preferred: Children's Nurses in the Old South." In *Neither Lady nor Slave: Working Women of the Old South*. Ed. Susanna Delfino and Michelle Gillespie. Chapel Hill: The University of North Carolina Press, 2002. 75-101.

Darden, Norma Jean and Carole Darden. 1978. *Spoonbread and Strawberry Wine: Recipes and Reminiscences of a Family*. New York: Doubleday, 1994

De Knight, Freda. *A Date with a Dish: A Cookbook of American Negro Recipes*. New York: Hermitage Press, 1948

Ferguson, Sheila. *Soul Food: Classic Cuisine from the Deep South*. New York: Grove Press, 1989.

Gilroy, Paul. *The Black Atlantic: Modernity and Double Consciousness*. Cambridge: Harvard University Press, 1993.

Gray White, Deborah. *A'rn't I a Woman? Female Slaves in the Plantation South*. New York: W. W. Norton, 1985.

Hunter, Tera W. *To 'Joy My Freedom: Southern Black Women's Lives and Labors after the Civil War*. Cambridge: Harvard University Press, 1997.

Inness, Sherrie A., ed. *Cooking Lessons: The Politics of Gender and Food*. New York: Rowman & Littlefield, 2001.

—. ed. *Kitchen Culture in America: Popular Representations of Food, Gender and Race*. Philadelphia: University of Pennsylvania Press, 2001.

—. *Secret Ingredients: Race, Gender, and Class at the Dinner Table*. New York: Palgrave Macmillan, 2006.

McFreely, Mary Drake. *Can She Bake a Cherry Pie? American Women and the Kitchen in the Twentieth Century*. Amherst: University of Massachusetts Press, 2001.

The National Council of Negro Women. *The Black Family Reunion Cookbook: Recipes and Food Memories*. New York: Fireside-Simon & Schuster, 1993.

Neuhaus, Jessamyn. *Manly Meals and Mom's Home Cooking: Cookbooks and Gender in Modern America*. Baltimore: Johns Hopkins University Press, 2003.

Nora, Pierre. "Between Memory and History: *Les Lieux de Mémoire*." In *History and Memory in African-American Culture*. Ed. Geneviève Fabre and Robert O'Meally. New York: Oxford University Press, 1994. 284-300.

Shapiro, Laura. 1986. *Perfection Salad: Women and Cooking at the Turn of the Century*. New York: The Modern Library, 2001.

—. *Something From the Oven: Reinventing Dinner in 1950s America*. New York: Viking, 2004.

Schenone, Laura. *A Thousand Years Over a Hot Stove: A History of Women Told Through Food, Recipes, and Remembrances*. New York: W. W. Norton & Co., 2003.

Shange, Ntozake. *If I Can Cook/You Know God Can*. Boston: Beacon Press, 1998.

Smart-Grosvernor, Vertamae. 1970. *Vibration Cooking, or the Travel Notes of a Geechee Girl*. New York: One World-Ballantine, 1992.

Spivey, Diane M. *The Peppers, Cracklings, and Knots of Wool Cookbook: The Global Migration of African Cuisine*. Albany: State University of New York Press, 1999.

Theophano, Janet. *Eat My Words: Reading Women's Lives Through the Cookbooks They Wrote*. New York: Palgrave, 2002.

Witt, Doris. "'My Kitchen was the World:' Vertamae Smart Grosvenor's Geechee Diaspora." In *Kitchen Culture in America: Popular*

Representations of Food, Gender and Race. Ed. Sherrie Inness. Philadelphia: University of Philadelphia Press, 2001. 227-49.

—. *Black Hunger: Soul Food and America.* Minneapolis: University of Minnesota Press, 2004.

Zafar, Rafia. "The Signifying Dish: Autobiography and History in Two Black Women's Cookbooks." In *Food in the USA: A Reader.* Ed. Carole M. Counihan. New York: Routledge. 2002. 249-62.

CONTRIBUTORS

Lia Blaj-Ward holds an MPhil in English from Nottingham Trent University and is currently approaching completion of a PhD at the Open University, UK, on the pedagogical framing of humanities doctoral students' experience of academic writing. She is involved in academic writing programmes and has presented papers on the relationship between humanities writing, (inter)disciplinarity and membership of academic communities of practice at conferences both in the UK and overseas.

Inga Bryden is Principal Lecturer in English and Head of Research in the Faculty of Arts at the University of Winchester, UK. She has published on nineteenth-century literature and culture, the Pre-Raphaelites, the Arthurian legends, the city in visual and literary culture, and Indian domestic space, and once curated an exhibition of paintings by contemporary British and Indian artists. Current research projects include an investigation of the meanings of Indian food in contemporary British culture. Unsurprisingly, her favourite cuisines include Indian and British, but also Italian and Thai.

Eleonora Chiavetta is Associate Professor of English Language and Translation at the Faculty of Arts of the University of Palermo in Italy, where she teaches Linguistics, English Language and Translation Studies. Her research focuses on discourse and genre analysis and on applied linguistics. Her latest publications include the monograph *Generi testuali e discorso specialistico: Writing for the Community of Gardeners* (Annali della Facoltà di Lettere e Filosofia dell'Università di Palermo, 2004). She has published numerous essays on in the fields of postcolonial literary studies, discourse analysis and genre analysis and translated into Italian various authors including Djuna Barnes and Vita Sackville-West.

Pere Gallardo-Torrano holds a PhD in English from the University of Barcelona. His thesis focused on robots as literary characters. For twelve years he taught at the University of Lleida (Spain), lecturing in English and American Literature and Utopian Studies. Currently, he is Senior Lecturer at Rovira i Virgili University, Tarragona, where he teaches courses on Literature, Culture and Science Fiction Studies. His research interests revolve around the influence of technoscience on Western societies. He has published in English, Spanish and Catalan. At present he is co-editing two volumes on utopian studies with articles which sprang from the 7th International Conference of the Utopian Studies Society held in Tarragona in July 2006.

Hélène Le Dantec-Lowry is an Associate Professor of American Studies at the University of Paris III (Sorbonne Nouvelle) in France, where she teaches American history. She specializes in African-American and women's history. She is the co-editor of *Formes et écritures du départ: Incursions dans les amériques noires* (L'Harmattan, 2000) with Andrée-Anne Kekeh-Dika, a book about migrations in the black Diaspora, and of *Ecritures de l'histoire américaine / The Writing(s) of African-American History* (*Annales du Monde Anglophone* 18, 2003) with Arlette Frund. She is currently completing an historiographical essay on the discourse on the black family in the United States, which will be published in Paris in 2008.

Miriam López-Rodríguez teaches in the Department of English at the University of Málaga, Spain. She is a member of the research groups working on American theatre there and was co-organizer of the international conferences on American theatre held in May 2000, 2002, and 2004. Her doctoral dissertation on Louisa May Alcott was published by the University of Málaga. She held a Fulbright Fellowship to study the Sophie Treadwell Papers at the University of Arizona, Tucson. She has co-edited *Staging a Cultural Paradigm: The Political and the Personal in American Drama* (Peter Lang, 2002), *Women's Contribution to Nineteenth-Century American Drama* (Servei de Publicacions de la Universitat de València, 2004), and *Broadway's Bravest Woman: Selected Writings by Sophie Treadwell* (Southern Illinois University Press, 2006).

Jopi Nyman is Professor of English at the University of Joensuu in Finland. His books include *Men Alone: Masculinity, Individualism and Hard-Boiled Fiction* (Rodopi, 1997), *Under English Eyes: Constructions of Europe in Early Twentieth-Century British Fiction* (Rodopi, 2000), *Postcolonial Animal Tale from Kipling to Coetzee* (Atlantic Publishers, 2003), and *Imagining Englishness: Essays on the Representation of National Identity in Modern British Culture* (University of Joensuu, 2005). He has also co-edited several essay collections including *Animal Magic: Essays on Animals in the American Imagination* (University of Joensuu, 2004), *eros.usa: essays on the culture and literature of desire* (Gdansk University Press, 2005), and *Reconstructing Hybridity: Post-Colonial Studies in Transition* (Rodopi, 2007).

Daniela Rogobete currently works as a Senior Lecturer at the Faculty of Letters, University of Craiova, Romania, where she teaches Intertextuality and Scottish Studies. She got her PhD in Postcolonial Studies and this continues to be her field of study. A particular focus of her research is upon issues of diaspora and exile as major factors in shaping and redefining national identities. She is currently involved in a project concerning the authenticity and legitimacy of diasporic writings in English, based on an analysis and redefinition of Indianness in the light of the politics of identity and the new remappings of political, geographical and cultural spaces. Her most important publications include *When Texts Come into Play—Intertexts and Intertextuality* (Craiova: Universitaria, 2003*)*, "Out of the Labyrinth: Textual and Visual Representation in Alasdair Gray's Short Fiction" in *Creadores de Evocation* (2005), and "Mapping Alternative Spaces" in *Euresis—(Post) Communisme et (Post) Colonialisme* (2005).

INDEX